I Have Survived

D1570303

I HAVE SURVIVED

One Woman's Ten-Year Journey as
a Breast Cancer Survivor

A Story of Hope, Courage, and
Resilience

Erin Arbabha

Copyright © 2013 by Erin Arbabha

All rights reserved. This book or any portion thereof may not be reproduced or used in any manner whatsoever without the express written permission of the publisher except for the use of brief quotations in a book review.

Printed in the United States of America
First Printing, 2013
ISBN 978-0615934617

Erin Arbabha
PO Box #2293
Stuart, FL 34995

ihavesurvivedbook@gmail.com
http://ihavesurvived.com

Editing and Interior Design
by
David Bernardi

davidbernardi@gmail.com

DISCLAIMER

The author of this book is not a doctor, simply a breast cancer survivor who has chosen to share her experiences. Before deciding on any course of treatment, readers need to check with their doctors. Some of the names and events have been modified to protect the privacy of those individuals involved.

To Mom and Dad

Contents

Preface

This is the story of my ten-year journey with breast cancer. I wish to share my story with as many people as I can, in hopes of helping other breast cancer patients and their families as they suffer through the emotional and physical turmoil this disease brings.

I am not a writer by trade. In fact, writing was always my least favorite subject in school. But in my opinion, writing is the best way to reach out to others and show them we are not alone. When I was going through breast cancer treatment, I looked everywhere for a friendly, easy-to-read, and to-the-point book that I could relate to. I didn't want to read anything that would bring me down, however—I wanted a voice that would energize and motivate me.

My intention in writing this book is to share the thoughts I collected while journaling during this period, so that others can find solace in my hardships and triumphs. If I'm able to reach only a handful of people, it will have been worth all the effort and then some.

I also want to recognize all the brave women and men in the world who are struck with breast cancer. (Sadly, many do not realize that men can also be afflicted by this malady.)

Finally, I wish to acknowledge all the mothers, fathers, sisters, brothers, lovers, and friends who remain by us when we need them. And let's not forget our beloved pets, who support us with their unconditional love when this is what we need most.

1

Mammogram

I wake up to the alarm clock around 6:00 a.m. I shower, drink a cup of coffee, and get into my car. With one hand on the steering wheel and another holding my coffee, I pull out of my street. Sandhill cranes are meandering across the yard as flamingos fly in the distance. I feel warm sunshine on my face, take a sip of coffee, breathe in the ocean air, look at the palm trees, and think just how lucky I am to live in paradise.

I moved to South Florida two years ago, leaving behind Midwest winters and my broken marriage with Jonathan. A large, prestigious Florida-based company had offered me a good income, a professional career, and a chance to live in paradise. I took it as a sign that it was time for a change.

Moving here on my own and starting a new career has had its ups and downs. But at this moment, I'm feeling happy to be away from the winter snow, and I'm enjoying this beautiful sky and sunshine in the middle of winter.

My Zen moment is interrupted by my cell phone ringing. It is my doctor's receptionist, reminding me of my annual OB/GYN exam this afternoon at 3:30.

I make it through my morning meetings. As the lunch hour approaches, I grab my gym bag and go downstairs to the company gym for my daily workout. I do a quick two-mile run on the treadmill, shower, grab a salad from the cafeteria, and take it back to my office to eat. Before I know it, it is 3:00 p.m.

When I arrive at my appointment, the receptionist tells me my doctor has had an emergency, and a doctor whom I've never met will be seeing me. *I'm going to have my annual OB/GYN with some doctor I have never met?* As I wait, I clench my teeth at the awkwardness, but I try to distract myself. They call my name; I'm very tense as I walk in. But when the doctor greets me, I am immediately impressed by his friendliness. *A doctor with a pleasant bedside manner—how refreshing!*

I casually mention the occasional pain in my left breast.

He is still reading my personal health history. "Has anyone in your family had cancer?"

I tell him my father's sister died from breast cancer at forty-two. The doctor asks when my aunt was diagnosed. I tell him that, as far as I'm aware, it was five years from her diagnosis to her death. He then asks me about the pain in my left breast. I feel more comfortable, because I'm getting so much attention from this doctor. Usually, my annual exam is a quick thirty-minute visit, and I don't remember the previous doctor asking so many questions. Maybe it's good to see a new doctor on occasion—a fresh look at everything, a different perspective. He asks me how long I have had the pain. I tell him the pain has been there since the previous August—five or six months, but I have been waiting for my annual exam to get it checked. He orders an ultrasound in addition to my regular annual mammogram.

I have had an annual mammogram for as long as I can remember. At each mammogram visit, I am always reminded of my aunt and how she was faced with breast cancer—how she was mutilated one breast at a time, with radiation and multiple surgeries almost forty years ago in Iran.

I walk into the testing area and register. The nurse calls me in, mispronouncing my last name, as always. (Over the years, I have learned not to make a fuss over it.) I change into a gown and walk into the mammogram room, which is cold and uninviting. The walls are a remarkably ugly gray. Just before the procedure begins, I start feeling very anxious. Again, I remember my aunt who lost her life to breast cancer.

The nurse puts my breasts inside the machine one at a time, squeezing them as if they are a dress being pressed at a dry cleaner.

"Hold your breath, squeeze, then breathe."

I do as I'm instructed.

We go through this routine for several minutes. She leaves to check the X-rays, comes back, and takes more pictures. I try to peek at her computer screen, but can't make any sense of it. Then she walks me into the next room for the ultrasound.

This procedure isn't as uncomfortable as the mammogram; however, the nurse performing the ultrasound has an unusual expression on her face, and it's making me nervous. Finally, she is finished and I'm happy to have all the tests completed. I get up, get dressed, and leave for the comfort of home.

The next day, I go to work as usual, with no thoughts about results. I have been having these checkups for the last fifteen years, and I lead a healthful lifestyle, so I have no reason for concern.

***

Friday, two weeks after my mammogram, I am ready for the weekend; I'm expecting guests from out of town. We have dinner plans for tonight. I arrive home around seven. As usual, I stop to check my mail. There is a something from the X-ray clinic, so I open that first. My eyes skim over the letter, expecting to see the same normal results I've seen for the last ten years. I walk into my kitchen, put the letter down, and as I walk toward the refrigerator to grab a snack, I get a sudden discomfort in my stomach. I pick up the letter to read it again, very slowly this time. I see the X-ray result marked as abnormal. I stand there, staring at the letter for a long time, and my vision begins to blur. The room begins to spin, and I'm feeling very dizzy. My first reaction is *Why didn't they contact me over the phone immediately? Why am I finding out about this in the mail two weeks later?*

I go through so many scenarios in my head regarding what this could mean. Reminded of how I have been experiencing minor pain and tenderness in my left breast, I start thinking about how my job has kept me so busy that I have ignored all the warning signs for the last six months. Even though the pain started back in August, I attributed it to the size of my breasts and the running.

The weekend goes by very slowly. All I can think about is my aunt, how I am doomed, and that this could very well be the end of my life. I worry about how this will affect my job and my independence. I don't have any family members here in Florida. I don't have any close friends here either, as it takes me a long time to develop close relationships. I'm very nervous and frightened. How am I going to share this with my family, who live more than 10,000 miles away, in Tehran, Iran?

I didn't feel comfortable sharing my fear and anxiety with my guests. I don't even know if I am capable of allowing myself to feel vulnerable. All my life, I have been told to be strong and never show weakness. My mother wanted me to be all that she couldn't be. I have always been admired for my independence, my confidence, and my figure. There has always been pressure to be perfect. My entire self-image is now threatened by the possibility of how things may evolve. It's enough to ruin my entire weekend.

I wait until 9:00 a.m. Monday morning to call my doctor's office. I talk to the receptionist and ask if I might speak to the nurse about my test results. In the most casual, robotic tone, she says, "The result is no big deal. Our office tried to leave you a voicemail. Your next step is to consult with a surgeon. The X-ray shows a small calcification the size of a grain of salt."

I am confused. Why do I need to see a surgeon for some stupid grain of salt showing up on my X-ray? I call

Dr. Ruiz, the surgeon, right away and get an appointment for the next day.

When I see the surgeon, he examines my breast and says the next step is to have a biopsy. A biopsy is a procedure in which a sample of tissue is removed from the body. A pathologist then examines the tissue under a microscope to determine whether cancer is present.

My surgeon recommends a "stereotactic" biopsy. He explains that this procedure is used to collect tissue samples from areas that contain micro-calcifications. In this type of biopsy, local anesthesia is injected prior to the procedure. The patient lies face down on a table with her breasts suspended through an opening, and X-rays are taken of the suspicious site from several different angles. A three-dimensional (stereotactic) picture of the abnormality is then created. A computer is used to guide the needle to the site to extract a sample.

I make an appointment for the biopsy; the earliest appointment I am able to get is in three weeks. It will be in the middle of the day, so afterward, I'll have to go back to work. I also have to go back to work now. But I am emotionally exhausted. How can I concentrate at work after all that? I think about how painful it will be to have to wait three weeks to find out the truth about what has been happening to my body. I feel overwhelmed. There is no one here to talk to about any of this. I haven't even told my parents, who live overseas, with no quick way to get here. I would not even know how to begin such a conversation with them.

I don't want to wait three weeks for the biopsy. I want to get to the bottom of this issue now. I decide to visit with Martha, the onsite nurse at my company, to ask for advice. Martha sees me right away, and after listening to me, she recommends another reputable local surgeon, Dr. Levy, with the hope I can get an earlier appointment.

I go home, ready to collapse from exhaustion after my day, which includes a daily 60-mile roundtrip commute. I sit numb on the sofa and the phone rings. It is Jonathan, my ex-husband. He tells me that he recently lost his job and has decided to take some time off before looking for a new one. He is coming to Orlando to visit his old friend Jack for a while.

I share the latest news with him. He becomes concerned and wants to come and help. I tell him it is not necessary. Everything is under control, but I will let him know if I need help.

The next morning I wake up, and all I can think of is which doctor I'm supposed to see today. I immediately call Dr. Levy, and to my amazement, he gives me an appointment right away. I go see him in the afternoon. He explains the various types of biopsies to me. Unlike Dr. Ruiz, he recommends surgical (excisional) biopsy. An excisional biopsy removes the entire mass or abnormal area until they have a clean, cancer-free margin, where no more cancer cells are detected. If there is a small suspicious area that is hard to find by touch, or if an area looks suspicious on the X-ray, they can target it precisely. After the area is anesthetized, a thin needle is inserted into the breast and X-ray views are used to guide the needle to the suspicious area.

"This is the best way to remove all doubt and get to the truth," the doctor says.

I cancel the stereotactic biopsy and make arrangements for the excisional biopsy this Friday. I am starting to feel down, since I don't have my family here. I start calling my friends in various parts of the country to let them know what's going on. I call my two brothers,

Jerome and Allan, who live out of state, and let them know about my surgery this Friday. Finally, I call Jonathan. When he finds out that I'm having surgery, all alone here, he says that he is on his way; he tells me I don't have a choice. I appreciate how protective he is of me. I'm conflicted about how to appropriately express my emotions.

<u>2</u>

Biopsy

MARCH 2002–APRIL 2002

It is Wednesday night. Jonathan is coming tomorrow. It gives me comfort that he is going to be here. As I am driving, I think about how quickly everything is happening. In spite of this, I feel a sense of calmness, although I'm not sure where it is coming from. Knowing there is a big ocean nearby feels comforting. Today, it's cloudy and windy with the occasional flash of lightning.

I make it through work on Thursday and come home early. Jonathan arrives late Thursday afternoon, and he gives me his famous teddy bear hug, lifting me off my feet. It's been almost a year since our divorce was finalized. We had many incompatibilities, but our major source of disagreement was that I wanted children and he did not. He is upbeat and very positive, as always. It is nice to see him, but the situation is bizarre; neither of us could have imagined being part of each other's life this way.

The first thing he says to me is "No matter what this is, we can fight anything." That gives me a burst of energy. Seeing his lack of stress actually gives me a burst of energy. His carefree, happy-go-lucky attitude sometimes annoyed me when we were married, but now I find it comforting. Should I let him help me? I put on a strong, independent front most of the time, because of the way I was raised, but this time it is different. I tell myself I am going to surrender and see what the universe has planned for me. It is the first time in my life that I truly feel out of control—or perhaps I have just now accepted that I have no control.

The next morning, we leave early for the hospital. The biopsy seems like it will be lengthy and complicated, but the nurses are kind and competent. The whole procedure takes nearly all day, but it goes well. The nurse tells me I will be getting the results a week later.

Since I was under general anesthetic during the surgery, I don't remember Dr. Levy at all.

Even now, I am not completely coherent. My thoughts are foggy and I feel drugged out. As soon as we get back to my house, I go to bed and sleep all night. The next morning, my left breast is black and blue, and is now the size of a small watermelon. I am so fearful that I call the hospital and speak with the doctor on call; he seems completely unconcerned with my case. I put ice on my breast, hoping the swelling will go down. There is also a great deal of pain, so I spend most of the weekend in bed.

I feel sad about where I am at this point in life. Two years ago, I left Iowa and moved to Florida for a new job and a chance to start a new life. Now I feel that I have gone backward. My ex-husband is back in my life, my left breast is about to explode, and there is no one else here to support me.

Monday morning, Jonathan goes to Orlando to his friend Jack's place. I get dressed and drive to work, although it is painful. My left side is aching very badly. I feel very sick and nauseated, but I have to go to work. I can barely move my left arm. The thirty-mile drive seems to take forever. While at work, one of my coworkers, a consultant, asks about the biopsy and why I needed to have it. Later in the day, I go to various meetings, and I am so distracted that I'm unable to concentrate. My worries are so much larger than the business discussions occurring around me.

Mid-morning, I receive a call from Dr. Levy's office. The doctor wants to see me right away. I ask if I can wait until Friday, but the nurse insists that I come today. Just before she hangs up, she suggests that I bring a family member. *What family member?* I have no family nearby. I wonder if "bring a family member" is code for "we are about to give you the worst news of your life." I leave work early and drive to the doctor's office alone. As soon as I walk into the small office, the nurses look at me; quietness fills the air.

I'm called into the doctor's office, where he is seated behind his desk. There are lots of books and papers and pictures of people I believe to be his family. He takes out a piece of paper and starts explaining DCIS—ductal carcinoma in situ, the most common type of breast cancer cells. He says they are pre-cancer cells in the body that are very likely to turn into cancer. He says the presence of these cells is what my biopsy revealed.

I ask what the next step is. He pauses and says we have to remove them. Then he starts drawing a picture of the breast and showing me how spread out the cancerous cells are—"there is one here, one here, another one here, one more here"—and pretty soon the paper is filled with polka dots. Finally, he says we have to do a mastectomy.

After that, I don't hear anything he is saying. My mind has gone blank and I start feeling dizzy. All I can think of is the mutilation of my aunt's body. I feel as though I'm about to faint. I ask for a glass of water, recompose myself, look at him calmly, and state that I'm not sure I want to do something this drastic. He writes down the names of two oncologists and suggests that I talk with one of them.

I get up and leave. Is he seriously asking me to have a mastectomy? I am so young, healthy, and fit. Even though he is a doctor, is he just another businessman who wants to make money? South Florida seems to have more than its share of medical businessmen like this. Who is he to tell me this? I have convinced myself that this simply can't be correct, and am now completely skeptical about this surgeon. I don't believe he is right; it can't be true. I'm going to get a second opinion for sure.

I leave the doctor's office not quite knowing what this all means. I have plenty of time to absorb the information while heading home. On the upside, the possibility of having a mastectomy is distracting me from the pain in my breast, which is still black and blue. I call Jonathan from my car to share the results. Then I call my brother Jerome. How can I tell my mother? Mom's health is poor and she won't be able to handle this. I keep driving, feeling like I'm in a trance, and I take the longer route home. I go by the beach, gaze at the ocean, and decide to stop at the local hotel eatery for dinner. I order the most expensive wine on the menu and steak, which I rarely eat, being as health conscious as I am. So much for good eating and healthful behavior. I find that I'm completely in the moment and actually enjoying the experience.

After I eat dinner, I drive home and go to bed, not really knowing what to think.

The next morning I rush while getting ready for work so that I can do the next logical thing and get in touch with an oncologist. I call Dr. Ray, who has been recommended by Dr. Levy, and get an appointment right away.

When I walk into Dr. Ray's office, I feel immediately comforted. She looks at my X-rays and reads the pathology report.

"I am not convinced that you need a mastectomy," says Dr. Ray. "It might be possible to resolve this with radiation."

I want to jump up with joy and hug her. "What do we do now?" I ask.

"I am going to contact Dr. Levy to discuss your case further."

I thank Dr. Ray and go back to work.

My cell phone rings an hour after I get to work and the caller ID reads "Oncology Department." I answer.

"Hi, Erin, this is Dr. Ray. I talked to Dr. Levy, and we were not able to agree on the diagnosis. We would like to do another biopsy."

I can imagine how Dr. Levy did not like Dr. Ray disagreeing with his diagnosis. Dr. Ray is young and new to the community. Who is she to question his judgment?

So, in order to settle their disagreement over my diagnosis, I am to have a second biopsy—and I still have my stitches from the first! This also means more time away from work, not to mention more pain, bruising, and anxiety.

After a while, I call Jonathan and give him the news.

***

It is Friday afternoon and I am at work. I have an appointment with Dr. Levy this afternoon to remove the rest of my stitches. It's been a week since my biopsy, and my breast is still swollen, and black and blue.

On top of this, everyone at work is feeling insecure due to upcoming layoffs. There is visible stress on everyone's face.

I wonder what I will do if I lose my job now.

I contact the HR department, explain my situation, and ask about my options for taking time off to have all these medical procedures. They recommend that I submit an FMLA form for the doctor to fill out. The Family Medical Leave Act (FMLA) is a United States federal law requiring employers to provide employees job protection and unpaid leave for qualified medical and family reasons. The bill was a major part of President Clinton's agenda in his first term. He signed the bill into law on February 5, 1993.

Jonathan picks me up from work for the appointment with Dr. Levy. The office is packed. Most of the patients in the waiting area are considerably older than I am. We sit and wait. Finally, they call my name. The surgeon seems tired after a week of work. As he removes my stitches, he asks me about my meeting with the oncologist, Dr. Ray, as though trying to get a different perspective on the conversation. I explain that Dr. Ray did not seem as concerned about the results of the biopsy. Dr. Levy does not appear pleased that a young, new female doctor questioned his judgment.

As I leave Dr. Levy's office, I give the FMLA form to the receptionist and ask her to sign it. I tell her that, under federal law, my job is protected when I take sick time off. She seems hesitant and confused, and appears to want to leave work without having to make any more decisions for the day; it is Friday afternoon, and even though it seems she could care less about my FMLA form, I press her to complete it. There is tension in the room, as many of the patients who seemed bored and depressed perk up. It's as if they are suddenly interested in my cause.

A nice elderly woman shouts from the other side of the room, "Hey, lady, this is federal law. It is not up to you! I can't believe you're working in this office and you've never seen this form before." Now I'm really getting anxious. It's been a long, tiring week, and I want to go home.

The receptionist looks at me and says, "Well, the only way you can do FMLA is if you are taking pregnancy leave or have a medical condition."

I try to be very patient. I look her in the eye and say, "Obviously I'm not pregnant. The doctor has removed a three-by-three-inch section of my breast, which has cancer cells. Now, *you* tell *me* if you consider this a critical medical condition."

Jonathan grabs the form from me, fills it in, hands it to her, and she signs it without making any eye contact. It is very tense. The receptionist seems nervous to the point of wanting to leave.

My second biopsy is scheduled for next week. I am still hopeful there has been a mistake with the diagnosis.

I hope that after the second biopsy, I can have a few radiation treatments and be done with the whole ordeal. That way, I wouldn't have to tell my parents a thing.

While we were growing up, Mom was very protective of both me and my sister, Francesca. She would not even let us pierce our ears, thinking that it might deform our bodies.

"Cancer" was a forbidden word in my mom's vocabulary. Cancer meant a death sentence or God punishing someone for something they'd done wrong. Normal, happy people just didn't get cancer; if they did, they kept it very quiet.

I don't want to shame my mother by telling her that her daughter has cancer.

***

Going for a biopsy is starting to feel like going for coffee. I know the process, the forms, and the routine. The second biopsy takes less time. I notice that immediately after this biopsy, I feel relief in my left breast. The hematoma and swelling are gone. The surgeon drained the excess blood.

I come home to rest. The next day, I get a call at around 10:00 a.m. from Dr. Ray, my oncologist. She sounds somber and apologetic, and that concerns me. I get out of my cubicle and step outside for privacy.

"I am now certain that you must have a mastectomy of your left breast," she says. "The cancer cells have spread, and after removing six centimeters of the surrounding tissue, they still do not have a clean margin. This is not a good sign. I am very sorry."

I sit in stunned silence for some time. Then I thank her and say good-bye. I'm feeling completely numb, unsure of what to do or where to go. Do I just go back to my office and continue trying to work? I keep wondering what is going on inside my body. I feel that I have an intruder inside that is destroying me. The more procedures they do, the more things they seem to find going wrong.

I go back to my office and try to concentrate. I still have lots of pain from yesterday's biopsy. The procedures have left me black and blue on the left side of my chest. I am feeling weak. Driving the thirty miles home is very difficult. I finally get home and think about calling my friends. I look at the list of names and numbers, and wonder who to call first. I realize at this minute that I know many people, but I feel comfortable calling no more than three on the list. That makes me sad—I have so many people in my life, but only three who I feel comfortable calling now. I'm thinking that my female friends might be more loving and understanding of my current situation and that somehow they might relate.

There is something surreal about making these phone calls, not knowing the stage of the cancer and how much time I have left. No word to my entire family yet, although I do call my brother Jerome, with whom I feel very close. As we talk, he stays calm and logical.

Meanwhile, Jonathan is visiting his friends in Orlando. When I call him about this ordeal, he says he will come back to stay with me. I'm glad that he is willing to help.

The next day, I tell my boss. Of course, his first reaction is "Oh my God … I'm so sorry." As soon as I hear the word *sorry*, I wonder if I should be feeling sorry as well, and then I get sad.

I think people mean well, but they just are not sure how to react when they hear such news. I don't want to hear people feel sorry for me. I want to hear people tell me it is a great fight, and that they are behind me and cheering for me and supporting me. The best help I get is from my long-distance friends, who remain strong and calm and offer to help throughout everything. I keep wondering how I am going to tell my parents. The thought of it makes me sick.

When I step into the shower the next morning, incisions and bruises remind me how fragile my body is becoming. Dr. Ray calls and wants to see me. I visit her during my lunchtime, and she breaks the news: I have stage I breast cancer and we have to do the surgery. She says there is no rush, but I should have it done in the next three months. Then she looks at me and says, "I'm sorry."

I go back to work, feeling pressured to share this with my family. Now what do I do? The doctor talked about the advantage of keeping one breast. She warned me that it would be more challenging to get sexually aroused with both breasts removed. I'm sure I gave her a look that let her know I truly could not care less about sex at this time. In fact, I decided at that moment that I didn't want anything more to do with my breasts. They had caused me so much agony.

***

I am finding it difficult to concentrate at work. I feel suffocated by doctors and nurses. All the doctors know each other, and I sense that the junior doctors feel pressure to agree with the well-established senior doctors. Why did I have to have two invasive biopsies in such a short period? Why so much pain and swelling? I am upset that I'm black and blue from the top of my chest to my abdomen, and that now I am being told I need to remove my entire left breast as well.

I still don't truly believe that I have cancer. How could I? I am too young and fit. I eat well and I haven't done anything wrong. So why am I being punished? It must be a bad mistake—poor judgment on the part of the universe. I am exhausted with all the thoughts running through my head. *I don't have cancer. It is all a big mistake. The doctors in South Florida don't know what they are doing. They are all wrong.* I keep repeating these words in my head. I want to run away.

Suddenly, I recall that twenty years ago I had a checkup at the Mayo Clinic in Rochester, Minnesota. It is one of the world's leading cancer clinics. I am going to call and see if I can get an appointment for a third opinion.

I call and explain my background, and I am immediately given an appointment. I finally get the courage to call my sister, Francesca, in Iran. She is my only sister and a year younger. We have lived apart all our adult lives yet had maintained a close relationship. We start our conversation as usual. I ask how Mom and Dad are doing and how her children are doing. We have our usual chitchat, and then I start getting her ready for the news.

"Remember how one of my breasts has been hurting since last August and how it has been uncomfortable to go running?" I ask. She says she remembers. "My recent X-ray showed a suspicious spot. I have had two biopsies."

There is silence.

"Well," I continue, "I have cancer."

She seems at a loss for words and then she bursts into tears. She is my baby sister, and all I care about now is to make her feel better. I tell her I'm planning to go to the Mayo Clinic for a third opinion. She is relieved. I make her promise me that she will not mention a word of this to Mom and Dad. I take a deep breath after I get off the phone and realize that was actually easier than I had expected!

The next day, my phone rings and it's Francesca. She confesses that she has told my older brother; now I'm getting worried. We talk and cry over the phone. I have been trying for the last fourteen years to get her a visa, so that she can come and see me in the United States, but I have not been successful. The thought that keeps coming up is that I am going to die without being able to see my sister in this country.

I arrange for a plane ticket to Rochester, as well as a hotel. I had asked for an appointment for two weeks from now, because I had wanted to be caught up at work before leaving.

I tell Dr. Ray that I am going to Mayo for another opinion. She prescribes me some anti-anxiety and sleep medicine to help me through the next two weeks. She is very encouraging, unlike Dr. Levy. When I had told Dr. Levy, he gave me a strange look and said, "People don't go to Mayo for something like this. This is just a routine mastectomy." I was furious. As I left his office, I met another doctor and mentioned Dr. Levy's comment. I said I thought he was being very insensitive. The doctor replied, "Dr. Levy would not have made that statement if it was his wife who had breast cancer."

***

Jonathan has gone back to Orlando, but he is in touch with me daily. My brother Jerome calls me at least three times a day. My brother Allan calls once a day, but tries to avoid discussing any medical issues. I also talk regularly to friends across the country. Elizabeth in Santa Fe calls me almost every night to express her support. She wants to come to Mayo to see me, but I ask her to wait and come later, when I have returned to Florida. I speak with Denise in Wisconsin every other day. She is coming to Mayo to accompany me on my appointments. My good, old friend Scott from Seattle calls me often.

I start realizing what is happening. I am getting myself prepared for losing me. Every night, I go to bed and tears fall uncontrollably. My eyes are constantly wet without me even realizing it. I feel a constant sense of grief, loss, and sadness. I get up every morning and go to work, but in the meantime I'm making plans for my departure from Florida. Every morning when I shower I look at my breasts, thinking how they are self-destructing and how the cancer may be spreading. I feel resignation, and I feel betrayal from my breasts. I'm preparing to say my final good-bye.

Then I remind myself that this is probably a false diagnosis and it will all be over soon.

3

Diagnosis

It is the night before my flight to Minnesota. I have to catch an early flight, but it is hard to fall asleep. I am flying there alone. Jonathan will stay behind and wait to hear from me.

Morning finally arrives. Getting to the Mayo Clinic in Rochester, Minnesota, from Stuart, Florida, is no easy task. I live forty-five miles from the airport, and there is no direct flight. I fly to Houston, change planes, and then fly to Minneapolis. After picking up my luggage, I have to get tickets for a shuttle from Minneapolis to Rochester, a seventy-five-mile trip. It is almost dinnertime by the time I arrive in Rochester on the shuttle. I check into the hotel right across from the building where I will have my appointment.

My good friend Denise, whom I have known twenty years, arrives shortly after I do. She looks worried but tries to be calm. We catch up, go to dinner, and then go to bed. There is too much unknown at this point, so we make it a short night.

The next morning, we get up early and go to the second floor of the hotel for a continental breakfast. I'm starting to get anxious. I stare at Denise and notice she is taking her time buttering her roll. I just want to go to my appointment, and it seems everything is moving in slow motion. I want to ask her how she can eat, knowing that I am in such turmoil, but then my rational side tells me to just sit and be quiet.

Downtown Rochester is where the main branch of Mayo is located. It is convenient, and I will be able to walk to my appointments. There is also an underground tunnel connecting the buildings.

The first stop at Mayo is the business office. I check in and show my insurance card. Mayo is covered as part of my plan. I feel so grateful to have insurance during this time of my life. Those who have no insurance are required to put down a deposit, the amount of which depends on the severity of the condition. The cost at Mayo is no more than at other cancer clinics, however. In fact, there are times when you pay less.

My insurance information is verified and validated. Insurance companies ask for volumes of information before they approve any procedure. One thing I have learned is that just because something is denied following the first request does not mean it will ultimately be denied. You have to be resilient and not quit when dealing with insurance companies. Mayo has an entire department that deals with insurance.

We finally arrive at the breast clinic and are greeted by a friendly receptionist. Everything seems nice and relaxed, which helps me remain calm. I see many younger women sitting in the waiting area. For a moment, I feel a connection with them all. I see fear, anxiety, sadness, and resignation in their faces.

There are people from all over the world—women wearing the Islamic hijabs over their hair, women wearing stylish outfits and carrying designer bags, and women with families. A young woman in her thirties has tears running down her cheeks, and she looks very anxious. I wonder if she has just received some bad news.

I start to feel anxious as I observe uncertainty, sadness, and fear on the faces. But I also see efficiency and harmony in the way Mayo handles patient services; I am impressed by the order and discipline to everything.

The nurse calls my name and escorts me to the doctor's office. Denise decides to go to the breast cancer library at Mayo to read. The breast clinic doctor is a beautiful, young Indian woman wearing a huge diamond ring. All I see are her deep eyes and the sparkle of the diamond. She arranges for me to have additional testing. They have my previous X-ray and a letter from the pathologist. She examines me.

I am still black and blue and bruised everywhere. She looks at me with horror and says this would never happen at Mayo. I spend the rest of the afternoon giving blood and having an ultrasound. I'm supposed to meet with the breast clinic staff at 2:00 p.m. to review my test results. One convenient advantage of the Mayo Clinic is that you can have your tests in the morning and meet with your doctor in the afternoon to get all the results. The staff is friendly and helpful, and there are volunteers everywhere to help the patients.

After my blood draw and ultrasound, I grab a cup of coffee from the clinic coffee shop and start walking through the main lobby. Everywhere around me there is artwork to admire. It makes me forget why I am here. Mayo has a large collection of beautiful modern art on display all over the campus. They even have an art tour for the patients and their families. The beauty that surrounds me captures my soul, and for the moment, I feel truly happy to be here.

When it is time, I report for my appointment and wait until they call my name. I'm feeling upbeat, ready to prove my Florida doctors wrong. Soon, I am called and escorted to the doctor's office. The first question they ask is whether I can get a copy of my original pathology slides and have them shipped there by priority courier. I call the hospital in Florida, finally manage to get the records office, and ask if they can mail my slides. Apparently, they are unable to locate my records. I shout, "How can this happen?" and hang up out of frustration.

I get called into Dr. Patel's office. After a few minutes, she walks in and calmly gets to the point. She doesn't bother discussing my test results. "You need a double mastectomy right away. The cancer is very aggressive, and you shouldn't waste any time. You have stage II cancer."

She continues, "Currently, the cancer is in your left breast, but we recommend prophylactic mastectomy of the right breast as well." The word *mastectomy* keeps coming back again and again. I have come all the way to Minnesota to avoid hearing this word, but I can't escape it. Also, it seems my diagnosis is getting worse by the day. I came to Mayo for a third opinion, hoping to find out things weren't as bad as they seemed, but now I'm being told that they're worse.

Still, it is not as much of a shock hearing it the third time. At this point, I am ready to surrender and stop fighting. I feel a sense of despair, sadness, and confusion.

Dr. Patel comes in and explains the procedure. There is no time to waste. The thought of my body self-destructing keeps coming back. I wonder what I did wrong to deserve this.

Dr. Patel leaves the room and Dr. Gartner, the surgeon, walks in with his assistant. "I am Dr. Gartner, and I will be performing the mastectomy operation," he says. I find him pleasant, with perfect manners. He puts me at ease instantly. He examines my breast and says, "We will be doing a skin-sparing mastectomy. This means the breast tissue will be removed through a small incision around the areola. The nipples and areola will be removed, but most of the breast skin will be kept, so that later on it can be filled with a breast implant."

The skin-sparing technique improves the cosmetic outcome and gives the best option for reconstruction. In a traditional mastectomy, however, much of the breast skin is removed.

Dr. Gartner is gentle and has kind eyes. The younger resident, however, is abrupt and emotionally cold, discussing my body as if it were some school project. As he talks, I suddenly feel tightness in my chest and have difficulty breathing. I feel dizzy and tears start falling uncontrollably. The young doctor stops talking and gives me a concerned look as I ask for a glass of water. I am feeling numb, but fortunately, my rational brain takes over, so that I can discuss plans with them. Dr.

Gartner recommends a bilateral double mastectomy, in which the right breast is removed prophylactically.

On the day of the surgery, one surgeon will perform the mastectomy, and once finished, the plastic surgeon will take over and do the initial reconstruction surgery. I am told my appointment with the plastic surgeon is later this afternoon.

I am also told they have already filed the surgery pre-certification form with my insurance company.

As I leave the doctor's office, I'm not the same person I was when I came in.

It is mid-afternoon. Denise and I walk back to my hotel room and make phone calls. I start with my boss and tell him about the urgency of having surgery. He is very understanding and supportive.

Next, I call Jonathan. I sense that he is holding back tears, but he starts cheering me up and telling me how we will fight this. I then call my brother Jerome. He listens carefully, without interrupting me, and then asks a few questions.

I get up and rush to my final appointment for the day. The plastic surgeon, Dr. Kanda, seems very familiar with my case, so I don't have to say anything. He starts by explaining my two options. The first, called TRAM (*transverse rectus abdominis* muscle-flap procedure), uses tissue from the stomach area, which is then implanted into the breast. He looks at my belly closely and tries to pinch.

"You don't have enough fat to qualify for this option," says Dr. Kanda.

"Oh, how flattering," I tell myself, "but just for the day, I wish I was fat."

He explains the alternative. "The second option requires multiple steps. After the mastectomy is performed by Dr. Gartner, we take over. A tissue expander with a valve is placed under your skin and chest muscle. During the surgery, we will inject a very small amount of saline into the tissue expander," he says. "After the surgery, every two weeks or so, two to four ounces of salt water will be added through a valve. This stretches the skin and tissue over a period of three to six months. Then the expander will be removed, and a salt-water or silicone-filled implant placed through the mastectomy scar and under the chest muscle to provide shape and volume. The goal is to make the breasts look as normal as possible. A few months after completion of this phase, we will build the nipples. After compete healing, which could take months, an areole will be tattooed around the nipples." Dr. Kanda talks about this as if he does hundreds of these surgeries a week.

The plastic surgeons and staff treat me as if there is a life after all of this is over. There is no talk about cancer for a change. They want to build breasts, creating a work of art that is as close as possible to the one given by my God. I have too much anxiety to worry about the aesthetics of my future breasts, so I trust the path I am following.

I am done with all my appointments today. Denise is going back to Wisconsin in the morning. We decide to go to Victoria, a local Italian restaurant, to relax. Denise is trying to be the best friend that she always has been for me. I see fear, worry, and anxiety in her face, but no words of that nature are spoken. We go back to our hotel and go to bed exhausted.

***

Today is my third day at the Mayo Clinic and I have my pre-op test, a meeting with the anesthesiologist, and a final appointment with the breast clinic. Denise left early this morning. Word must have spread fast at work, because I start getting phone calls.

I go to Starbucks and then head across the street to the Gonda Building, one of the newer buildings at Mayo, which is decorated with beautiful modern art. Outside, there are rows of colorful tulips. The air feels fresh, and I sense a revived energy, as if everything is going to be okay.

I take a sip of my hot soy latte as I enter the Gonda Building. Inside, a patient is playing a classical piece on the grand piano downstairs. I feel hypnotized by the beauty of the art and architecture. Everywhere I look, there is art—on the walls, even on the ceilings. I lose track of time and realize that I need to go or will be late for my appointment with the anesthesiologist.

First, I have to stop at the business office to start the process of getting insurance approval, which is no easy task on its own. The doctor has to complete a form that lists, in detail, every procedure that will be performed. The business office then matches each procedure with an associated code.

The information is sent to the insurance company, whose underwriter examines and questions every procedure. Mayo business works on the patients' behalf, interacting directly with the insurance company to get pre-certification approval before surgery. For this and many other reasons, the Mayo Clinic has made a lasting, positive impression on me.

After the business office, I report to the breast clinic to review all the logistics of the surgeries. Dr. Patel greets me and tells me with amazement that the insurance company has approved surgery for only one breast.

"They require a thirty-day waiting period before they can approve the other breast, since that is a prophylactic procedure and not considered an emergency," Dr. Patel says with a shocked expression. She is very upset, because the idea of doing one breast and waiting thirty days to the other breast is an inefficient use of resources and will end up costing more, not to mention threaten my health by requiring two major surgeries in a thirty-day span.

Dr. Patel faxes a letter to the insurance company explaining the medical necessity of approving the surgeries for both breasts. She tells me that we have to wait. They go ahead and plan the surgery for next Tuesday, hoping everything will be approved by then. Today is Thursday.

***

It has been twenty-four hours since Dr. Patel faxed the letter to my insurance company. I am stuck in a Rochester hotel room all alone. I have completed all my tests, surgery is scheduled for Tuesday, and I still don't know if my insurance will cover both breasts. All the insurance papers have been filed, Mayo has made an emergency scheduling exception, but there is still an issue with the insurance company's approval.

I call Stan, my good friend, who works for the corporate communication division of my company. I ask if he has any ideas about getting in touch with the right person at the insurance company, so that they can expedite the approval process.

"Don't worry, let me see what I can do," Stan says. I have been friends with Stan and his wife, Diane, since I moved to South Florida. They have both been very supportive. The first time I met Stan, he told me he was from Wisconsin, and there was in instant connection between us. Running into people from the Midwest is like going home, considering I lived there for so many years.

There is nothing left for me to do this morning. I am anxious about whether the insurance company will respond in time for the surgery. To escape, I leave and go shopping.

So what do you shop for if you know you are scheduled to have your breasts removed? Definitely not clothes. I am thinking ahead again as I walk mindlessly through the store with a hollow feeling and what I imagine is a sad, anxious expression. I see the pink-ribbon store and walk in. Sarcastically, I think, "Well, this is going to be a treat." They have an undergarment for the day after a mastectomy, with Velcro on the side so you won't have to raise your arm to put it on. (It takes about a month after the surgery before you are able to raise your arm completely over your shoulder.) The bra has these fillings for breasts. I touch it and almost faint. Just the thought of giving up part of my body and replacing it with foreign matter makes me nauseated.

I am very uncomfortable being in this store, but I decide to buy the undergarment. What else should I be looking for? I keep walking. There are lots of patients and families. As I walk into a jewelry store, I feel sad and confused. The luminous light reflected from the most beautiful brilliant crystal necklace catches my eye. I believe crystals are magical—I love how a crystal lets you see all the colors of the rainbow even when it is dark inside. I touch the crystal necklace and feel its illumination inside of my body and spirit. For just a moment, I feel the darkness in me being replaced by the beautiful colors of the rainbow. I buy the crystal necklace and hold it in my hands as a reminder that there is light in my life.

I keep walking, see a bookstore, and decide to go in. I start looking for books on cancer and hardly see anything. I want something that can help me make sense out of everything that is happening to me right now. I don't find anything that appeals to me, so I leave the bookstore and keep walking.

It's almost lunchtime. I walk back to the Gonda Building and go to the lobby downstairs. There are many comfortable sofas and breathtaking works of art.

An older woman sits down at the piano and starts playing. Someone who might be a patient walks to the podium and starts singing opera. I have never been to an opera before. I look up and see this grand, black sculpture of a man in a position of prayer. The opera singer's voice penetrates my heart and comforts me. For a moment, I completely forget why I'm here. I glance at the tulip garden and see all the people sitting and listening to the beautiful music. I am fully present in the moment and the only thing that matters is *now*. I feel the presence of God everywhere. I see doves flying in the atrium garden. As I hold onto my crystal necklace and gaze at its glitters of light, the tears start falling down my cheeks, but I don't feel sad. I feel an inner peace and knowingness and strength, as if a divine universe is pouring a surge of energy into my heart. I don't feel scared anymore. I know at this moment that everything will be okay. I feel surrounded by the energy of pure love.

I go back to my hotel room, feeling energized and focused. I am not even thinking about the insurance company. I walk into my room and lie on my bed, holding my crystals and looking at the refracted light.

It is 3:00 p.m. Friday, and the phone rings. I am not expecting any calls. A polite male voice introduces himself. He's calling from the executive customer service office of my insurer. My heart begins pounding.

"We just want to let you know that your surgery has been approved."

I pause and then ask, "You mean for both breasts?"

"Yes, of course!"

I'm ecstatic, relieved, and grateful! I tell him, "God bless you!" To this day, I am not sure what Stan did, but I am grateful for his help.

***

It is the night before surgery. I am clutching my crystal beads anxiously, trying to see some light. I'm trying to keep all negative and scary thoughts away. I'm determined not to allow any darkness into my soul.

By now, Jonathan has driven up from Florida, Jerome has flown in from Colorado, and Allan has driven in from Iowa to be here for my surgery. I still haven't spoken about this to my parents, although they have heard about what is going on from my older brother. I don't have the heart to call them yet; I want to wait until after the surgery. We all go to a Greek restaurant for dinner. My brothers try to make me laugh, to keep my mind occupied so I don't dwell on the surgery. Of course, they are successful; they know me so well, and I love them for that.

4

Double Mastectomy

MAY 2002

At 6:00 a.m., we walk into registration, and a nurse shows us where to go. I try to keep out all emotion and think only about the tasks I must do now to get to the next step. Everyone is nice and professional. The staff seems knowledgeable and helpful, and many kind and willing volunteers answer questions and support patients and their families. I go through the standard procedures of completing forms and answering questions. Then they take me in at around 11:00 a.m. My friends and family are asked to wait in the guest lobby.

In the locker room, I put on the hospital gown and place my belongings in the locker provided. The nurse comes in and escorts me out. I'm feeling anxiety about what is ahead, but I try to hide the emotion and not appear weak.

My brain is busy with thoughts of what is to come. I know that one of today's procedures will determine whether the lymph nodes are affected. Before the procedure is performed, they will inject the tissues around the tumor with a blue dye and a radioactive substance. This substance will travel to the sentinel nodes. The sentinel lymph nodes are the first lymph nodes to which cancer cells are most likely to spread from a primary tumor. The surgeon will then make an incision in the axilla, where he can pick out the nodes, which turn blue with the dye. The blue dye and the radioactive tracer are used to help identify the sentinel nodes, which are not always easy to find. The pathologist then will examine the cells in the sentinel nodes under a microscope.

I am taken to a room before going into surgery. It is the recovery room. It is dark and quiet. I see patients in various states of consciousness. Everyone speaks in whispers. I lie down on a bed and wait as directed. It feels like something from a dream.

The anesthesiologist, the mastectomy surgeons, and the breast reconstruction plastic surgeon all come in. They speak to me in low voices and ask questions. They all try very hard to keep me at ease. I trust that they will take good care of me. After I meet the entire staff, I wait until it is my turn for the operating room. Finally, two of the nurses push my bed toward the doors; suddenly, they open and we are in the operating room. It is freezing cold. Everyone is wearing a mask. I recognize my nurse and feel comforted by her. I am very scared, but my fear does not last long. They place the IV in my arm, and I watch as it drips, drips, drips...

***

I wake up with tightness and burning in my chest. The nurse informs me that I am in the recovery room. The surgery has taken six hours. I tell the nurse I'm nauseated, so she injects me with anti-nausea medication; in a short while, the medication seems to be taking effect. It is very quiet in the recovery area, and nurses are speaking in whispers.

As they move me out of the recovery room, I look over and see Jerome, Allan, and Jonathan. They look anxious but relieved. The surgeons have told them that the tumors were successfully removed and that there are no traces of cancer left. Even though I can barely open my eyes, I feel like a conquering warrior. I am supposed to remain still for twenty-four hours, so I do. I want to touch my chest to see how it feels after having both breasts removed, but I don't. I'm frightened about what I will find, and I don't want to inadvertently affect what the surgeons have done so carefully. The uncertainty surrounding the outcome of the operation scares me, but somehow I am able to sleep—the pain medication is apparently working.

When I finally open my eyes, I see Jerome, Allan, and Jonathan watching me. They all smile, and I feel very comforted. I ask them if the doctors were able to remove all the cancer, and they all say yes. I'm elated that I won't have to have chemo because all the cancerous cells have been removed. Jerome comes closer. He looks at my chest with his typical analytical curiosity. I ask him to tell me how bad it is. I don't have the heart to touch it myself. He bends over to look more closely. I am concerned about how he might react. He peeks at the incisions under the bandage. He doesn't seem surprised or concerned. I am comforted by his reaction.

"It looks great," he says. That is not exactly what I was expecting to hear.

I find enough courage to touch my chest. Surprisingly, I'm neither shocked nor frightened. I touch my chest again and it is flat. This is such a strange experience. I can barely recall when I was without breasts, and even if I could, I know I wasn't concerned about it in the least at that young age. Now, having gone from a D-cup to a completely flat chest, it seems surreal. Under both arms are holes through which drainage tubes let out excess fluid and blood. The nurses clean out the tubes several times a day. Even a slight movement of the tubes in my body causes excruciating pain. I attempt to raise my arms; they are heavy, as if boulders have been tied to them and are holding me down. My upper arms feel as though they have been pinned to my ribs. I'm able to move my fingers and my wrists, however, and can bend my elbows a bit. I'm grateful even to be able to do this much.

The breast reconstruction will have to be done gradually: in my case, over a span of two years. At the time of the mastectomy, they put in an empty, temporary implant with a magnetic valve. Later on, the doctors will be able to locate the valve from outside the skin by detecting the magnet. They will very gradually inject saline into the valve to stretch the skin and muscle in preparation for the permanent implants that will replace these temporary ones.

During the first twenty-four hours, I sleep most of the time. My mastectomy surgeon, Dr. Gartner, comes to see me early the next morning. My plastic surgeon, Dr. Kanda, checks in on me shortly after. They both appear confident and project a positive attitude; this comforts me and gives me hope, even though I still feel worse than I've ever felt before in my life.

**

The day after surgery is the first day that I have to get out of bed and walk. Moving is the last thing I want to do. Regardless, the nurse comes in and tries to help me sit up, then stand. I feel sick and start vomiting, but she remains calm, as though this is just part of the routine. I sit back in the bed for a few minutes until my head and stomach are calmer. Then we try again. I'm holding onto the pole that has my IV with one hand and onto the pole that holds my urine bag with the other. My head is swimming and I feel tightness and pain in my chest. I'm unable to move my arms. Any slight movement brings on excruciating pain, but the nurses are very helpful, and we start walking. I take one little step, then rest, another step, then rest some more. The five-minute walk feels like a five-hour triathlon. I'm exhausted and keep thinking *I can't take this pain!* I can't stand up, and I feel as though the pain might just kill me.

I'm finally back in bed and receive more morphine, so I sleep. Next, the nurse removes my catheter and I am able to go to the restroom. The nurse waits. When I am finished, she says that I need to clean up. I look at her thinking, *I have to wash my face and brush my teeth, but I cannot move my arms. How am I supposed to do that?* It seems like the most challenging task of all. I tell her it will be much faster if she helps, but she says time is not an issue.

Doing things the same way as I always have will not be possible. I can still bend and use my fingers, legs, toes, and teeth—but nothing else. She turns on the water and hands me a washcloth. I walk toward the sink and barely reach the running water, just to get my hands wet enough. It becomes obvious to me that I will not be getting a lot of pampering. According to the nurse, the Mayo Clinic believes in self-sufficiency. I am suddenly thinking about my mom and how she would always stand back and watch me. She was always proud of me, and though she never expressed it, I know we've always had a special relationship.

Now that my hands are wet, how do I reach my face? Then I think to bend over. All those years of yoga come in handy, and I am able to touch my face with my wet hands. I grab a toothbrush and I can lift my arms, but only high enough to touch my teeth with the toothbrush, and I am done. This whole exercise takes about two hours, but I feel empowered afterward. Then I go back to bed.

***

It is 10:00 in the morning on the third day after the surgery. Dr. Kanda and his young residents come into my room and they all look very nervous. I am feeling good, and wondering what is going on. The doctor wants me to show my chest to the students, but he is being respectful and wants to make sure I am comfortable in front of these strange young residents. I look at them and say, "Let me stand up so you can see better." Under my robe, all I have on are my panties. I tell myself that my breasts are gone, so there's no need to be shy. I stand up and take off my robe. Two long tubes hang from my underarms, which are clipped to my panties. I look at the residents, put my hands on my hips, and—with my chin up—I say, "Okay, gentlemen, what do you think?" That breaks the ice, and they smile and look at each other. I now know that while my body may be weak, my spirit is strong.

I sleep most of the day, waking up only a few times. I am told that on Friday, the fourth day after my surgery, I will be leaving the hospital; they are apparently very serious about the self-sufficiency aspect of their program. I am exhausted, but I am ready.

***

Today, I will be released from the hospital. My hotel room is a short walk from here. The nurses bring a wheelchair into my room to get me ready for departure. It is hard to believe everything that has happened in less than a week. I am so drugged with pain medication that I am numb to emotion. The nurses tell me that I have an oncology appointment on Monday. I look worried and then I'm told this is a standard post-op visit after this type of surgery, so there's nothing to be concerned about.

They put me in the wheelchair, give me my release documentation and my prescriptions, and then Jonathan, Jerome, Allen, and I leave the hospital. The first stop is the hospital pharmacy to refill my pain medication. Then we return to the hotel.

I am feeling remarkably good. Everyone, including me, seems pleased. Jonathan and Jerome are staying in the same hotel and will be here for another couple of days. Jonathan will be rooming with me to provide around-the-clock care.

***

As soon as we get back to the hotel room, I want to talk to my mom and dad. I dial their number. They know I have had this surgery. My father answers, and as soon as he hears my voice, he chokes up and starts crying. He tells me I can have anything I want. He tells me not to worry about anything. He also says not to get stressed out. "We are all here for you," he tells me.

Even over the phone, I sense his anxiety and his kindness. Then he hands the phone to my mother. I try to comfort her. I wish her a happy Mother's Day and tell her I'm feeling great.

***

I am expected to have the drain tubes attached to me for two weeks. Meanwhile, I cannot move my arms, and the drains need to be cleaned every two hours. There is so much blood and other fluid coming out of the breast area, I feel nauseated every time I look at it. Any slight movement of the drain tubes causes searing pain.

I am in and out of sleep most of the weekend. I wake up when it is time to take pain medicine or when the drain cups need to be emptied. There are cups, or containers, at the end of the drains that collect blood and fluid. They have to be emptied several times a day. And sometimes they are clogged, making the procedure very tricky and scary. You must have complete trust in anyone doing the cleaning, as they have to squeeze the tube as they run their fingers over the entire length of it. I trust Jonathan and feel very comfortable with him. I am grateful he is here with me.

I wake up Sunday morning at 2:00 a.m. with agonizing pain in my chest. The pain is so awful that I cannot even sit still in bed. I get up, take my medicine, and pace the room back and forth. I am howling from pain. Jonathan is acting agitated and trying to sleep. I'm sure he does not appreciate being woken up, but my drain tubes need to be cleaned and I need help. I lie still like a helpless infant as he cleans the tubes for me. I am *so* uncomfortable and in *so* much pain. The pain medicine finally takes effect and I fall asleep at around 6:00 a.m. As soon as I do, there is a knock on the door. My brothers stop in to say good-bye. They have to get back to their jobs and lives. Since Jonathan is not working, he can stay a while longer.

I wake up when it is time for more pain medicine. I wake again when it is time for the drainage tubes to be cleaned. My sister Francesca calls from Iran and wants to talk. She is upbeat and relieved that everything went well. I feel that she is here with me.

Elizabeth from Santa Fe, Denise from Wisconsin, and Scott from Seattle also call to express their support and love.

***

It is Monday, the third day since I was released from the hospital. I have an appointment with the oncologist. I am told this is a routine visit after the surgery and before I'm discharged to go home. The oncology department is very busy. I check in, sit, and wait. The room is an eclectic mix of people—old and young, with and without hair, and some in wheelchairs. Some appear to be completely lost within themselves. I am relaxed and pain-free at the moment, as I have finally figured out when to take the pain medication for the best effect. I must stay one step ahead of the pain and take the pill before the pain is there.

Finally, the nurse calls my name. I am taken to a private room. In a warm manner, she starts explaining that the pathology lab indicated one of my lymph nodes was positive and showed microscopic traces of cancer. Therefore, they are recommending six months of aggressive chemo.

My body grows progressively numb the longer she speaks. I hear things like "losing hair," "early menopause," and "drastic side effects," like my hair never coming back. I wanted to shout, "Fuck you!" because I am stunned that this is happening, after running to the finish line and celebrating my surgical victory. Now I realize this is just the beginning of my continuing nightmare. I am told chemo must start three weeks after the mastectomy.

Jonathan and I go in to see the doctor. The oncologist, whom I've never met, is a short, stocky, middle-aged doctor with no trace of human emotion. He asks me to get ready for the examination and then starts discussing the treatment. At this point, there has been enough time for the news to sink in. I'm still angry, so I ask him how much experience he has had in this field. I'm in total denial and do not want to believe that I have to have chemotherapy. In my mind, that is only for people in the movies or those who are dying. I'm fine. I have already had both breasts removed. How much more can I take?

The doctor gently responds that he has thirty years of experience, so I sit down and pay attention. He also mentions that he has a daughter my age and he would tell her the exact same thing: "You are too young to die. We want to make sure that we remove all microscopic traces from your blood." He then asks me the name of my local oncologist.

Some of the side effects of chemotherapy are low white and red blood cell counts, hair loss, memory loss, mouth sores, neuropathy, watery eyes, fatigue, loss of appetite, increased chance of infection, and in some cases weight loss or weight gain.

The amount and the type of chemo received at each session depends on many factors, including the patient's height and weight, overall health, and the type of cancer. Generally, an onsite chemotherapist determines the exact dosage and schedule for chemo treatments. I am thinking, *Why don't you just kill me now and get this over with?* I am so discouraged.

I return to the hotel room. I have to call my family and let them know about the chemo. I'm so hesitant to call. I now feel as if I have to put a positive spin on chemo, so they won't feel bad, but I have no energy to make them feel good about the situation. I call Francesca, start sharing my day, and tell her right away that I have to have chemo. She is stunned once again. Not sure what else to say, we just say good-bye. By now, I am exhausted. I take some pain medication and go back to bed to rest. When it is time to clean my drain, I wake up. For the next two weeks, this is my routine—mine and Jonathan's.

During this time, I decide to get a very short haircut, and I start mentally preparing for the next challenge. I see Dr. Kanda several times, and he looks pleased with the results, but I look at my nude body with disbelief. I have scars and lots of loose skin on my chest. I'm very scared when I walk, because I don't want anyone to run into my chest. I have a hard time believing this surgeon will make me look normal.

I also get cards and gifts from my friends at work and around the country, and I appreciate every one. It is so wonderful to just stay in bed and read my cards. I feel love and energy coming into me with every letter that is written. Somehow, word has apparently gotten out that I have cancer, because I am also getting cards from friends of friends, whom I have never even met. I then get a book titled *Maiden Voyage* from a colleague. It is about an eighteen-year-old girl who decides to sail the world alone. I can relate to her story.

***

It has been three weeks since I was released from the hospital. Today, I have my final appointment with Dr. Kanda, the plastic surgeon. My doctor removes the drain tubes and I feel some relief. It is time to go back home. I happen to stop at the gift shop after my appointment and come across the cutest stuffed white polar bear. I have to have it. I name him Fluffy. That night, my last at the hotel, I put Fluffy on my chest as if he is hugging me as I fall asleep. I become instantly attached to Fluffy. He is warm and has an innocent feel about him.

Jonathan drives back to his mother's farm to get some of his things and bring them back to Florida. He is going to stay with me for the duration of chemo. Flying home alone is a challenge. Walking from one terminal to another and going through security is exhausting.

I hold Fluffy in my lap as the plane takes off. Earlier, I called my friend Miles to ask for a ride. He greets me at the airport and drives me home. It has been a month since I left for Mayo to get a third opinion. I had left thinking I had stage I cancer, but then found out it was stage II. As Miles and I arrive home, my neighbors are all there to welcome me! I really appreciate that I have such good neighbors.

A little later, there is a knock on the door. It is my next-door neighbor, bringing me groceries. A few minutes after that, another neighbor brings a big dish of lasagna and a bowl of salad. I can't help thinking I'm all alone and scheduled for chemo the following week, but they are all so generous, and I'm touched by their kindness. Jonathan is driving down from Illinois to help me with chemo, and my good friend Elizabeth from Santa Fe is taking ten days of personal time to be with me while I go for my first chemotherapy treatment. I'm overwhelmed with love and care from my friends and neighbors.

I wake up in a great mood and play some of my favorite music loudly. I sing along. I stand in front of a mirror and look at the horrible scars and what appears to be the beginning construction of new breasts. I love belly dancing, so I play some middle-eastern music and start doing the movements in front of the mirror. I get carried away with some of the movements and forget about my damaged body. Suddenly, one of my incisions looks as if it may be coming open. I freak out, stop, and ask myself, "What are you doing?"

I will not allow the damage of my body to wound my soul. Though I've pursued careers in the more rational fields of science and engineering, I have always been drawn to art. I am learning that art is my way of fighting the feelings of panic and despair that have come into my life with cancer, and it works beautifully for me. I am reminded of a poem my dad gave me, which I had framed and which hangs in my bedroom. Translated, it says, "Creativity, beauty, and art are the only way to fight death." I remember the day he and I were in Tehran in a bookstore; he saw the poem on the wall and asked the storeowner to write it down for him. He gave it to me, and I've had it framed and kept it all these years to remind myself of its truth. That was almost twenty years ago.

5

Chemotherapy

JUNE 15, 2002–NOVEMBER 8, 2002

It's a Thursday, and Elizabeth is coming to spend ten days with me. I'm going through my first chemo treatment tomorrow. An artist, writer, scholar, and teacher, Elizabeth has been my friend for more than fifteen years. She has a very calm and serene demeanor and is able to put me at ease when I'm in her presence. She has lived more than five years in Japan and practices transcendental meditation, calligraphy, and tea ceremony. Elizabeth and I have always been kindred spirits, sharing intellectual and spiritual conversation.

Jonathan and I drive to the Palm Beach airport to pick up Elizabeth. She looks artsy as usual, with short, spiky black hair and pale white skin.

I have a neighbor stopping by tonight, and Elizabeth and Jonathan are in the kitchen preparing food. It feels like we are having a party. I am not sure what to think about all this. I don't feel like having a party. I don't want to socialize. I just feel like going to bed, being left alone, and not waking up. It bothers me that even though I have not completely recovered from the mastectomy, the doctors feel that I am strong enough to start chemo. I take my anti-anxiety medicine and go to bed early.

***

Elizabeth, Jonathan, and I are expected to be at the hospital's chemo treatment center by 10:00this morning. As we get ready to leave, everyone looks nervous. I hold on to my crystal beads and try to remain calm and unafraid. I have no idea what it will be like. All I know about the experience is what I have heard. Somehow, my long-standing, deep-seated fear of injections makes me more nervous today than on the day of my surgery. It's one reason Elizabeth is here.

We walk into the hospital, register, and go through the typical insurance-filing. We wait and then are greeted by the nurse. She walks us to the infusion room, where there are recliners, small TVs, and IV machines everywhere. So far, so good. I was expecting some bizarre, scary place, but this is okay. The pharmacist comes in, asks me how much I weigh, and explains the combination of chemo drugs they will be giving me.

"Your chemo order from your doctor is for a six-month period. The first three months of chemo will include Adriamycin and Cytoxan (AC), and the second three months of chemo will consist of Taxol."

AC is also known as the "red devil," due to its color, and because, when injected into the vein, it burns. Also, it is highly toxic, and it turns the urine red for five hours after treatment.

Taxol is a plant-based anti-cancer drug. It is an irritant that can cause inflammation of the vein and a severe allergic reaction. If the medication escapes the vein, it can cause damage. Due to the possibility of a severe allergic reaction, patients generally require large doses of steroids prior to Taxol chemo treatments. Of course, the steroids themselves can have numerous adverse side effects.

The nurse inserts the needle into my wrist, while Elizabeth reminds me to exhale as much as I inhale, and coaches me to look steadily into her eyes. Chemo begins. I start feeling coldness in my vein, since the Adriamycin is cold. At the same time, there is a subtle but persistent burning. I tell myself, "So, this is what it feels like to be poisoned." Gradually, I fall asleep.

It is about 1:00 in the afternoon and time to leave. I start paying attention to all aspects of my body to see how things feel, and so far I don't see many changes. I am told that my urine will be red after the first injection, and it is. Apparently, that is evidence that everything is working on schedule. I have read over and over about chemo and have even visualized it. The experience is not as scary as I originally thought. Having two close friends sitting next to me is helpful. They are like my cheerleaders, watching me go through this event. They are kind, caring, and attentive. I will always remember having them by my side when this war started.

We walk out of the hospital and get into the car. As I sit in the front seat, I begin to sense changes in my head. It feels like a bad hangover, then being on a high-speed rollercoaster. The motion of the car makes the feeling worse. My stomach still feels okay, since I was given an injection of Zofran for nausea. We get home and I go straight to bed.

The ring of the doorbell wakes me. It is about 6:00 p.m. I get up to answer the door and it's my friend Kristin; she's brought matzo ball chicken soup for dinner. Elizabeth and Jonathan seem very at home while enjoying the soup and socializing. Kristin and I met two years ago when we were judges at a local high school science contest. We quickly became friends. Kristin and her family treat me as though I am family. I'm invited to every family event.

We finish eating, and I get up to go to my bedroom to find an air mattress on the floor. It appears Elizabeth and Jonathan have worked out the sleeping arrangements for the next ten days. I have only one guest room, where Jonathan has been staying. Elizabeth will be using the guest room.

The next day, I am still feeling okay and seem to have some energy. Elizabeth suggests we go to downtown Stuart for lunch. I am able to eat a bagel without any difficulty. We stop by the beach and walk on the sand for a few minutes. Then suddenly I'm tired and feel ready to sleep. I keep telling myself this is not bad at all, considering that I have not thrown up yet. We come home and I head straight to my bedroom.

***

Three days after the first chemo treatment, I can barely open my eyes. I am feeling so tired. Even breathing is painful. I breathe very carefully, taking small breaths in order to avoid pain in my chest. I feel so helpless and guilty for letting Jonathan and Elizabeth do all the household chores. Though I have not had as much nausea as I did the first day after chemo, Jell-O has become a regular item on my menu.

I am scheduled to return to work in about a week. I have been told my hair will be gone within two weeks after starting chemo. Elizabeth takes me shopping for clothes. My closet looks dark, as it is full of business suits. We go to the mall and she helps me pick comfortable, loose-fitting, bright, cheerful clothes that I can wear to work. Our next stop is the wig shop. I have too much fun at the wig shop, trying so many different colors. None of them is perfect, but I am able to pick the exact color and hairstyle I want.

***

Today I have an appointment with the local plastic surgeon, Dr. Latino. It has been almost one week since my first chemo. I feel tired most of the time and my skin is starting to look grayish. I will have saline injections in my temporary implants (tissue expander) just about every two weeks until they are fully inflated. The breasts are inflated gradually, so the muscle has time to slowly stretch and expand.

The doctor reads my file. Then a magnetic device is placed on my breast, close to the port. Once the port is located, they inject the saline through the port. The pain afterward reminds me of severe sunburn.

This week I get several calls from friends all over the country. My sister calls me once a day from Iran. She is so upset that she cannot be here to take care of me.

Jonathan, who is currently taking a break between careers, feels that he is supposed to be here and that a divine force has brought him to take care of me. I am grateful for his help and generosity, but I resist him every chance I get. I don't like how he has just moved in, considering that I left our marriage a year ago. I feel guilty that he is here taking care of me, and I ask myself what that means. Does he expect something from me? Is he being nice to me with the hope of getting back together? I tell him that I'll be fine, but he has always been very protective of me, and we have always remained friends. He simply is not going to let me go through all this alone.

***

It has been over seven days since my first chemo. I have not lost any hair yet, but my skin is still gray and I have dark circles under my eyes.

Elizabeth left today. That and being so far away from my family brings me down. I often feel sad and isolated. I get in my car and just drive. I take Kanner Highway, and after about fifteen minutes, I find myself in downtown Stuart. I notice an art studio that I hadn't seen before and decide to stop in and check it out.

Class is in progress. The art teacher has long, beautiful blond hair and an angelic face. She walks toward me and welcomes me to her class. I tell her that I have had surgery (with no details), and I want to paint with my left hand. She smiles as though no further words are needed. Then she introduces herself as Renee and immediately leads me to an easel with a blank canvas resting on it. She provides me with acrylic paints and explains her three-step process for painting a picture of an orange. I look around the room to see what the other students are doing, and then I begin my first painting. For several minutes, I completely forget about everything going on around me and only experience the art. The last time I felt this way was when I was at the Mayo Clinic looking at artwork. It was such a powerful feeling.

My spirit is overwhelmed with joy after I complete my painting. After class, I go to pay her; she refuses to accept anything, but I insist. She makes me feel as though merely being at her class is what mattered. She tells me that I will be her guest and can come to class as often as I'd like. I feel so blessed by this experience.

***

It is two weeks since I began chemotherapy. According to the schedule, I should be losing my hair today. I go to the bathroom and start brushing my hair. Then I decide to find out if it will come out if I pull it. To my amazement, it does—wow! At first, I think this is interesting, so I start pulling and keep pulling, as though I am pulling weeds out of the garden. I call Jonathan to come and see. His face turns pale and I know he is not sure what to say. I keep pulling and then I look in the mirror. I look like a chicken with its feathers plucked off. I cannot believe it. Reading about it and experiencing it are completely different. In my head, I knew what to expect, but going through it is devastating. This is yet another one of the most traumatic moments of my ordeal. Without saying a single word, I begin to cry. I wonder what is next. With no hair and no breasts, two major symbols of femininity, I begin to wonder what I am. What class do I belong to now? I certainly don't feel like I'm a woman. Jonathan comes over and says, "That's enough." He suggests that we shave my head, so we do, and now I'm officially bald.

The next few days, every time I look at myself in the mirror, I get angry. My head seems to keep growing, the longer I look at it, and it just keeps getting bigger and bigger. I'm consumed with the thought that my head is a monster that is eating me alive; but then I try to smile and it softens it up a bit. I don't want to leave the house, because it is such a hassle. I have to wear sunscreen on my head now. Meanwhile, the tissue expanders are growing inside my chest, and I have a bulge under my blouse so I can pretend to have breasts.

I can't get used to being bald. I call Francesca and tell her what has happened. I am looking at myself in the mirror while I am talking to her. I start crying and telling her how hard all of this is and how there seems to be no end. And just when I feel that I have touched upon all of the ugliness surrounding my situation, something else hits me: Francesca is hurting as she hears me cry out in so much pain. In the meantime, I am looking at my face in the mirror. I look like a scary cartoon character. She keeps talking to me, trying to lift my spirits. She has never spoken to me this way before. *She reminds me that I am a child of God and I am light.*

"You don't fight darkness with darkness. You bring light," she says.

I am now looking at my reflection and talking to her as though there were three people here: me, my sister, and the something or someone else—perhaps spirit, light, God within me. The more I look into my eyes, the less of my physical self I see. I am connecting to a beautiful force, energy, light, spirit, God—or, love. All of a sudden, I find myself in the most beautiful place. I feel at peace and connected to all living beings. I am surrounded by light, energy, and love. At this moment, whether I have hair or no hair, breasts or no breasts, chemo or no chemo, cancer or no cancer, it doesn't seem to matter. I am surrounded by an array of the most beautiful light. I am having a conversation with the divine. I don't want to go back to my physical body.

Having no hair makes me feel cold. Every time I shower, the first touch of water on my head makes me shiver. Showering with no hair is quick, however. I don't need shampoo, and I don't need to shave—all I need is soap. It is the middle of a hot Florida summer and I am constantly freezing. I find an old ski cap and put it on, and I never let it out of my sight. I also find a small flannel blanket. Both of those things are very comforting to me.

***

Today is the first day of July and I am going back to work for the first time since I left for Mayo. This is the third week since the first chemo treatment. I want to appear normal and avoid any unwanted attention. I wear my short auburn wig and some of my new clothes: a turquoise colored top and khaki skirt. I have plenty of time during my commute to work to rehearse in my head the process of walking into the building and using my security access to enter. I wonder if my security card even still works.

I get to the parking lot and park in the same place as always. For a moment, it reminds me of the last time I parked here and how the world was so very different for me then. With some difficulty, I get my laptop and my bag out of the car and walk toward the building. I still have some weight restrictions, so I need to be careful. I insert the security card and the light turns green. I try to go through the revolving door, but part of my handbag gets stuck and it takes some maneuvering to get through. I get to the lobby, hoping to catch the escalator to the second floor, but as usual it is broken. I take a detour to find another elevator.

Finally, I am walking toward my cubicle and see my nametag still on the wall. That is comforting. The light on my phone is blinking, indicating I have voicemail. I am unable to check my voicemail, since my password has expired; I call the help desk to have it reset. After getting situated, my coworkers start dropping by one by one to welcome me back. Miles walks by and waves. He almost looks reassured that I have made it back and look well. Lisa brings me a Welcome Back balloon and a box of chocolates. A couple of vice presidents have heard that I am in, so they come by and give me a hug. I tell everyone about my chemotherapy.

The more the day progresses, the more I talk to people, and the more depressed I get. Everyone looks visibly stressed. I hear rumors of layoffs next week. The word *layoff* used to scare me, but now it doesn't seem to have the same effect. Perhaps, it is the sleeping and anti-anxiety medications. I think everyone is shocked at how great I look. Some people express disbelief at my medical absence.

Finally! My first day back at work is over. The wig has been bothering me. I feel like I'm getting blisters on my scalp. As soon as I get in my car, I take the wig off and replace it with a scarf. I sigh, relieved as I start driving home. Driving thirty miles seems like a challenge, but I try to stay focused.

At last, I am home. Jonathan seems anxious to talk about my day. He's been home all day and doesn't have a whole lot to say about his own day. He has dinner ready. He looks a little depressed and unsure about things, but coming home to find him here does comfort me.

***

Before my second chemo treatment this Friday, I go back to Dr. Ray, the oncologist, for blood work. This is a routine visit that is common during chemo treatment; the chemo does a great job of killing blood cells. It's been two weeks since my first dose, so the oncologist tests my blood to measure the white and red blood cell counts. If my counts are below a certain threshold, I will receive an injection to bring up the levels before the next chemo session. I'm beginning to feel like a lab animal with all the testing and the chemicals being pumped into my body.

I end up having to get an injection of Procrit to help with a low red blood cell count. I do this on my lunch break one day, then return to work. I have very little energy, but not working isn't an option. I have to work to pay my medical bills, my mortgage, and all the other bills I am still getting from my surgeries—and now, bills for the chemo treatments.

One day, I look at the bill from my recent chemo and I can't believe how high it is. The insurance company has been good so far, except for a few denials. One thing this experience has taught me is not to accept a denial by an insurance company. I always write a letter, stating the facts and proving why a procedure is necessary. I never call them on the phone. It is important to have written documentation when dealing with insurance companies.

In addition to all the medical bills, my kitchen table is piled high with envelopes—bills for water, electricity, telephone, cable, home insurance, car insurance, and so on. A stack of unread mail continues coming every day. I'm fatigued and in survival mode and not able look beyond my immediate physical needs. Simply seeing the pile of unopened mail increases my anxiety.

**

It is the Wednesday before the July 4 weekend, and I'm due for my second chemo session on Friday. My surgery is now about two months behind me. My chest muscles are stretched to a point where my breasts now look like a D-cup. The skin on my chest is thin and sensitive.

I drive home from work and find Jonathan all dressed up and ready to go out to dinner. We go downtown and eat at an Italian restaurant. The food is fine and it is really pleasant to be as far away from work as possible. I have my first glass of wine after three months. Jonathan is enjoyable and seems at peace. I relax and reflect a bit.

As I think about it, I realize that I somehow find getting out of bed, getting dressed, and showing up for work comforting. It adds necessary structure to my days and makes me feel as though I am still in the game and have not given up—I'm just experiencing a temporary setback.

The next morning, however, I wake up feeling miserable. It is hot and humid. My street feels deadly quiet. I feel so depressed and lonesome. I miss my parents, even though I receive phone calls at least three times a week from them, as well as from siblings and friends. My mind feels dark, as though I'm lost in a long, dark, foggy, endless night.

I do my yoga routine, then call my sister Francesca in Tehran. As I complain about my bald head, tears start falling. She keeps telling me how much she loves me, how she would do anything to kiss the skin of my bald head, how she would hug me and would never let go.

***

Today, I'm going for my second chemo treatment. I am not as afraid as I was during the first treatment. I now know what to expect.

There is so much going on in my body. I had my period this morning, and it is light. I wonder if this is the beginning of early menopause, which I was told might occur. I have been experiencing regular hot flashes lately. This isn't what I need just now— something else to distract me and disrupt my sleep.

Jonathan and I check into the hospital. My name is called, so we walk back into the infusion area. I am directed to a corner where there is a recliner, a small TV, and an IV at each chemo station. There is a chair next to each recliner for the patient's guest. I sit down and a nurse walks in to greet us. She starts by sticking the IV needle into my hand. It takes several attempts to find my vein. I begin to panic each time she misses. She is finally successful and starts the red devil, then switches to Cytoxin. I fall sleep after the start of the IV. I hear someone offering crackers. I open my eyes and see a volunteer with a basket. The IV machine makes a unique sounds when the chemo ends, which wakes me. I open my eyes. It is time to go home.

**

Two days have passed since my second chemotherapy session, and I've been feeling horrible the whole time. I feel stuck in my body, in this house; even Jonathan seems to be feeling suffocated with everything. I try to look on the positive side, but I'm just not sure where that is. I don't know where my life is going. I wonder about my relationships with everyone and how they really perceive me. It's hard to know for sure, but I trust my friends and family unconditionally—they have always been there for me when I need them the most— they are the most important people in my life. They all have their own lives to lead, so I don't get to see them as much as I'd like. I miss my family terribly. I don't like being alone and stuck here in this house. I am starting to feel worse and worse as the days pass.

The third day after chemo I ask Jonathan to take me to the beach to breathe the ocean air as a reminder that life is still here. We go to the bookstore in the afternoon. I find solace in books. I find a book about breast cancer with a photo of a bald woman on the cover. I feel depressed just looking at the bald head, so I move to the diet and health aisle. Learning about what is happening in my body gives me understanding and a sense of control. I have always found reading enjoyable, but being sick gives me permission to relax and not feel guilty about doing it—or about doing anything. I feel free to explore, write, and paint without time constraints. My life is whatever is *now*.

***

I have been feeling more nauseated than after my first chemo. Dr. Ray has prescribed Zofran, which gives me relief, but it wears off too quickly. I have read that the side effects of chemo get progressively worse as your body weakens. I now agree with that. I don't have much of a sense of taste anymore. I can't eat anything solid. I am only able to digest Jell-O and drink tea. I also enjoy having chocolate milk shakes. Food feels as if it is stuck in my stomach for hours. My digestive system is not working well, and I am always cold. The nausea is the worst thing to deal with. I also cannot sleep at night, and I am getting night sweats.

Dr. Ray tells me that I'm going through menopause due to the chemo. She prescribes Prozac to help fight the side effects. The last period that I had was the last period I would ever get, and freezing my eggs was not an option prior to chemo. I'm heartbroken, sad, and overwhelmed by a sense of loss. I'm one step closer to death and will never experience the joy of motherhood.

Nights seem so long and endless. I just open my eyes and stare at the ceiling, hour after hour, until I finally fall asleep. I feel an intense darkness that I have never experienced before.

***

Today, I receive a call from an old boyfriend, Edward. Edward was a tough, successful Wall Street investor from New York, with a lavish lifestyle and expensive taste in sports cars, Champagne, Cuban cigars, and women. This is the first time he has called since he learned about my cancer. He says he has been reluctant to talk about my breast cancer and didn't want to face me and see how I was beginning to change and how I looked. I've had a difficult time understanding his reaction. He used to project a strong, tough exterior but now seems unable to have a simple conversation about cancer.

He tells me he had a heart attack two weeks ago and had to have triple bypass surgery. I find the timing so bizarre. Here I am, back at work after two rounds of chemo, when I get his call. I now realize how naïve I was to believe that all that equaled power. *Once again, I am reminded how unpredictable life can be.*

***

I look like so many other cancer patients. Wherever I go, people immediately notice. Most people are kind and courteous; they treat me with care and dignity.

I receive a call today. My two brothers, Jerome and Allan, are coming for an extended visit. I'm excited that my brothers will be with me, but they really don't know what to expect.

Jonathan and I arrive at Palm Beach International Airport to pick up Jerome and Allan. As soon as they arrive, they start teasing me to try to get my mind off the cancer, but it doesn't work; I'm feeling moody and don't take the teasing well. I don't have any energy and just want some tender kindness. They are both kind, but this is very uncomfortable for them, and I know they are trying their best.

They go grocery shopping and cook some of my favorite foods for me. Time speeds by. Before I know it, it is Sunday and time for them to leave.

I am really feeling awful. There is an intense heat inside me that feels as though it is bursting to get out. It feels like fire. I am having night sweats. It is the start of menopause. I am thirsty all the time. I have no sense of taste. I am getting blisters all over my skin. Even going to the bathroom is painful. My skin has become so thin that it is easily irritated. I eat cold watermelon, which helps to cool me down.

***

It is Friday morning and we are due at the infusion room at 10:30 for my third chemo treatment. We are still in the AC cycle. I am weak and wonder how much longer I can take this. I walk in and lay on the recliner. The nurse comes over and starts poking me, looking for a good vein. She injects the red devil manually and then sets up the IV for Cytoxin. Within thirty minutes, I fall asleep.

I open my eyes and it is 1:00 p.m. Jonathan takes me home, and before going inside to collapse in bed, I check the mail. I see a box with my name on it. I bring it into the house and open it. It is a box of the most beautiful, luscious peaches that I've ever seen! I read the attached note; it is a gift from my old friend Scott in Seattle. He has signed me up for the Fruit of the Month Club. What a thoughtful thing to do! Scott had always been there for me, a close friend of mine for almost twenty years. Scott has a very high-energy personality. Normally, I can easily keep up with him when we have conversations, as we quickly move from one topic to another. However, during chemo, when he calls to talk, it takes a tremendous amount of energy just to chitchat. Even talking on the phone is becoming more difficult. I thank Scott and then go to bed.

***

I'm going down fast. I am losing weight and look yellow and gray. I have no hair anywhere. My temporary implants are inflated every other week, and this is very uncomfortable. My energy level is gradually declining. The first three days after a chemo session, I am in bed most of the time, but I lie awake. It is like sitting on top of a volcano and observing the fire and turmoil inside, but not being able to do anything about it. The longer I observe the fire, the more I am able to make friends with the fire. I don't get angry. I watch and pay attention. I usually have my crystals by my bedside. The multitude of color in them brings a glimmer of joy to my spirit.

My routine now consists of chemo every three weeks, with two days off from work. I have a blood test on the Thursday before chemo; if my cells are within an acceptable range, I go for the next chemo treatment. If the range is not acceptable, I receive a Procrit injection. Also, as part of the routine, I continue to see the local plastic surgeon every two weeks for saline injections in my implants. After each visit, my chest feels like a balloon that's ready to burst, until my skin stretches and adjusts to the added volume.

Every three months, I fly to Rochester for my checkup, which consists of a blood test, chest X-ray, and plastic surgery evaluation. One day I sit down and add up the number of times I've been poked by a needle. I come up with a ridiculously large number—more than two hundred times in the past six months! And it's costing me a great deal of money! The medical bills just keep coming and coming, and they are piling up. I never realized how expensive chemotherapy is. I am dealing with the insurance company regularly. I keep very detailed records, having learned that when you have a dispute, you need a written record. I have to write letters to the insurance company to make sure that my bills are paid on time. My mind seems to be working well, and I'm making good decisions so far. I always know what needs to be done—I just need help with the execution.

***

More than two months has elapsed since I started chemo. I have lost so much weight. I'm all skin and bone, and I look yellow. They are continuing with chemo despite how fragile I am. I ache and feel restless all night.

One night, I can't sleep, so I get up and crawl outside. The sky looks colorful with the moonlight and the stars. I am in awe of the beauty, and I imagine that, if there could ever be a rainbow in the dark, this is what it would look like.

Despite being so tired and weak, I sense a special magic. It actually feels as if the stars are talking to me. These days, I don't question anything. I don't know what normal is anymore. The stars seem to be telling me a story about a rainbow. I sit down on the porch, smile, and listen. Without realizing it, I've fallen asleep and am having a wonderful dream:

Once there was a rainbow named Glow who loved to play and be mischievous. Every day when the sun came out, Glow and her mother would leave their home and spread their wings across the fields and the river, watching the children play.

One time, Glow, feeling playful, got lost and was left behind. The sun had disappeared and Glow was losing all her colors. She started crying, her big tears falling and forming a puddle, which turned into a pond. The tears would not stop, and they were getting bigger. Glow looked down and, to her surprise, she saw a River, but she continued crying.

The River, unable to take any more water, said, "Stop it, my child. You will be fine."

Glow jumped as she saw her own reflection; she could barely see herself. The River looked at her and she only then realized that the River had spoken to her.

"Have faith and follow me," the River said. "I will help you find the Land of a Thousand Suns, and you'll be a much bigger rainbow than you have ever been."

Now energized, Glow decided to go with the River. The River started flowing and Glow went along. They saw a Tree that was barely alive, and as soon the Tree saw the River coming, it became excited.

"At last," screamed the Tree. "River has arrived and I will live."

"Come with us," said Glow to the Tree. "We are on our way to the Land of a Thousand Suns, and can you imagine what you will become when you have all that light."

The River welcomed the Tree. Now the Tree and Glow flowed slowly with the River, trusting the river. The night was dark, but there was a full Moon. The Moon saw its reflection in the River and thanked the River for helping her see her own beauty.

"I had forgotten what I was," said the Moon to the River. "Thank you for reminding me and reflecting back at me."

Glow, Tree, and River continued on their journey. Glow saw a couple of Plant Seeds just waiting. As soon as they saw the River, they became excited.

"We have been waiting so long for you to arrive!" they said.

River kept flowing, with Glow and Tree following. The night was long. The stars were shining, watching River. What a glorious and beautiful night. Glow was not crying anymore; she was so looking forward to seeing the Sun. She put her trust in River and kept following River. Soon the night appeared to be ending, as they glimpsed the light. River began to flow through a tunnel, and light was fighting to get in. Glow, Tree, and River made it through this narrow tunnel and emerged into a land of beauty: a giant sky full of light. Glow's color started to return, and she became a great rainbow. Tree began to grow too. River smiled at them.

Glow now realizes that she does not need to be afraid of the dark any more. She now sees the beauty of darkness. She realizes there is no such thing as light and dark—they are connected, there is no night without day, and they each have their own beauty.

I open my eyes and Jonathan is there, watching me.

"Say, you've been here for the last two hours. I was getting concerned. Are you okay?"

"Oh," I tell him. "I haven't felt this good for so long…"

***

It has been almost three months since I started chemo. My nausea is spinning out of control. The Zofran isn't working. Sometimes I can't even drink water without getting sick. Today, I have to go to our Miami office for a two-day training session, so I arrange for Jonathan and me to stay at a hotel. After checking in, Jonathan drops me off at the office for training and goes back to the hotel. The Miami office is old and dusty. I feel a sinus headache coming on, which could be due to an infection. I contact my doctor, and she calls in a prescription at the local pharmacy. She prescribes sulfa antibiotics and a codeine-based painkiller. I take the medication that night. My head hurts so badly and I'm getting even more nauseated. There is an intense, burning pain at the base of my skull.

The next morning, I realize our rental car smells like cigarettes, aggravating the nausea even more. We have an eight-mile trip home. I am hoping this nausea will calm down. There is nothing worse than nausea. I start vomiting what looks like clear water, since there is nothing in my stomach. The vomiting continues nonstop from Miami to West Palm Beach. Once there, we check into an ER and they do a CT scan to make sure I am not having a stroke. (I'm not.) After the scan, as we are leaving, we walk by the infusion center where I get my treatments. The familiar smell of the treatment room and the sound of the buzzer on the IV make me so nauseated that my legs become weak and I fall to the floor. It is at this moment that I realize how sad it is when cancer takes away your dignity.

We come home and I go to bed. As the nausea persists, my doctor prescribes marijuana pills. I start taking the pot pills to fight the persistent nausea; they seem to help. I am looking very skinny, but my temporary saline implants look huge while the skin is being stretched. I have a wig in the Jackie O style, but I am very thin and my breasts are huge in comparison. If it weren't true, it would be funny to tell people I've had cancer and a double mastectomy, since everyone stares at my chest as I go about my day.

***

Today, I say good-bye to the red devil, as I'm scheduled for my last AC chemo treatment. After today, I'm 50 percent done with my chemo. I look like a dying patient; I'm all skin and bones, with yellowish flesh and dark circles around my eyes. I avoid looking in the mirror. I am treated differently wherever I walk. People get quiet when they look at me. Some people are respectful and honor me by the way they look at me, and some just avoid eye contact.

Today is a special day. I'm feeling proud that I have made it this far. Coming to the infusion treatment center is like coming to visit my family. With all the bald patients, I feel at home here.

I have completed four rounds of AC chemo and I'm due for my three-month checkup with my plastic surgeon and oncologist at Mayo. My oncologist has told me that 80 percent of cancer reoccurrence takes place in the first two years after treatment. I will have to have a checkup every three months during this first year, every six months during the second year, and annually after that.

***

It is the night before my trip to the Mayo Clinic for my three-month checkup. I have completed three months of chemo and am officially done with AC. I'm filled with anxiety. The night seems endless, cold, and dark. I have an early flight. I get out of bed at 4:00 a.m. and jump in the shower. Jonathan drives me to the airport. I'll be making this trip alone.

With much difficulty, I finally make it through airport security. I fly to Houston, change planes, and fly to Minneapolis, arriving around 6:00 p.m. I get into the Rochester shuttle and discover that I'm sharing this ride with a doctor and several patients. I feel the camaraderie in the van. I am not afraid to say that I have cancer, because the person sitting next to me may have something worse. It doesn't make me feel any better or any worse—just human. This makes the ride to Rochester easier to bear.

I check into my hotel and it already feels like home here. I spent a month at the hotel when I had my surgery. Still, at night, I feel nervous being in the hotel room all alone. I hold my crystal close and look for its lights, and that comforts me a bit. I try to distract myself with a work-related project, some graphic design for a website I'm working on. I find creative work calming.

Finally, exhausted after a long day of traveling, I get ready for bed, since I have to get blood work first thing in the morning.

***

Today I will know for sure if the chemo has been working. Every blister, pain, and ache makes me wonder what is happening in my body now. Just recently, I started getting painful blisters on my eyelids. In addition to Dr. Big, the oncologist, I have to see Dr. Kanda, my plastic surgeon.

I start the day with blood work, followed by chest X-rays, then I report for my appointment with my plastic surgeon. He starts examining me and his expression is one of an artist looking at his latest design. They take pictures of my breasts to monitor the progress of their formation. He decides to inject saline into one to make sure they are symmetrical in volume. My breasts are sore from the injection. This usually lasts for a few hours until my skin is stretched. He tells me that we will do the next surgery to insert the permanent implants sometime in March 2003, which will be about ten months after the mastectomy. By then, I should be fully recovered from all the side effects associated with chemo.

It is 11:00 a.m. and I'm done with all my appointments except oncology. I am not able to relax until I get my oncology test results. I go to the Mayo Cancer Center to wait for the appointment. I find many resource materials there, including books, papers, Internet, and videos to help educate patients. I always feel that walking in there shines some light on this dark, horrible thing. The more I read about it, the better I feel. Just knowing what is happening helps open my eyes.

Finally it is 2:00 p.m. Time to visit my oncologist and get the test results. Dr. Big has a sense of humor, although he has a very solemn demeanor. It is hard to read him. You never know what news he has had to communicate to the previous patient. He walks in and, first thing, apologizes for being late. He shows no emotion. He starts with light conversation. Perhaps, he's wondering why I have come all the way from Florida alone, considering how weak I am. He asks me to undress so he can examine me. I can't take it any longer and I abruptly interrupt.

"How was my test result? Am I okay? Is the chemo working?"

He pauses and says, "Yes." That is all I need to hear. While he is examining me, I start going through my lengthy list of questions and he patiently answers all of them. I am reminded how much I hated him the first time he told me I had to have chemo, but my emotions are much different now. I see how much he cares, and I feel a bond with him.

Dr. Big is very concerned about the blisters on my eyelids and schedules an appointment for me to see a specialist right away. This doctor puts me on antiviral medicine immediately and tells me I should be grateful that the infection didn't get into my eyes.

After my positive report, I let out a deep sigh. I go to Starbucks and treat myself to my usual soy latte. I call Jonathan, Jerome, Francesca, and Allan. My sister always lets everyone in Iran know the results.

Every time I come to Mayo for a checkup, my family is a wreck. My older brother, David, and his daughter, Sonya, are here in Rochester and plan to meet me for dinner tonight. I'm looking forward to seeing them.

***

Three months have passed and I'm finished with the first set of treatments (AC). I look terrible, feel weak, and have dark circles around my eyes. My skin still looks grayish yellow. I have blisters on my tongue and my skin is breaking out. I also have sores on my back. It is time to get ready for my new treatment. About three months to go. The new chemo treatment is called Taxol, and I have been warned that it may cause allergic reactions.

Because of the allergy risk, I have to take steroids for at least three days before the start of the treatment. These chemo infusions will take four hours, because they have to be done slowly. My face looks bloated and puffy due to the steroids. I walk into the infusion room as if I'm going into the local coffee shop. I recognize some people and we say hi to one another. Some people look old and sick. Good thing they don't have mirrors here. I keep telling myself that I don't look that bad, but in my heart I know I really do. Mental lies are good sometimes to protect us. What a depressing place. I try not to think about it. I feel like I'm stuck somewhere between life and death.

The nurse starts the IV and tells me they have to do this treatment very slowly due to the deadly allergic reaction it may cause. Somehow, it is comforting that when I hear the words *dangerous* and *deadly*, I don't panic like I used to.

As soon as they start the infusion, I fall asleep. I wake up a few times and see volunteers walking around, serving crackers to patients. I hear a woman having a conversation in the background. She is talking about her date this weekend. *How can she think about dating right now?* I wonder, and I fall asleep again. I open my eyes and it is 2:00 p.m. and time to go home.

As soon as Jonathan and I get home, I go straight to bed and sleep until 9:00 p.m. I wake up for a couple of hours and then try to go back to sleep, but it turns out to be another restless night.

I wake up the next morning and have this incredible rush of energy. It is probably from the steroids. To my amazement, I go to the garage, find my bike, and go for a ride.

Later that morning, I am not nauseated, but my mouth tastes strange and feels like it is burning. I feel dehydrated. My bones start to ache. After speaking with my doctor, I begin taking 250 mg of vitamin B6 daily to help with the joint pain.

***

Work has been therapeutic for me. People at work are very understanding, but I sometimes find myself in awkward situations. One day, I had a meeting with a project manager, and as soon as I walked into her office, she took out hand lotion and started moisturizing her hands. The scent immediately made me nauseated, and I had no choice but to get up and leave. I later went back to her office and tried to explain. She looked at me as though I had intentionally been rude.

Another time, I was in a meeting with five men late in the afternoon. As soon I walked into the room, I could smell their body odor and aftershave. I became sick. I felt as if I were in a jungle with a bunch of animals. The other day, I received flowers at home and had to get rid of them. Any scents or odors immediately make me sick. I notice that the infusion center uses coffee as a deodorizer. Unexpectedly, the smell of coffee is quite pleasant.

**

My brother Jerome is stopping in on his way home from a business trip. He always leases a car when he comes down, and drives himself to my house. Jerome is a great cook, and he makes pasta for dinner.

The next morning, we drive to the beach and then go to the coffee shop. He never once looks at me as a sick person and never treats me like one either. I like it, but sometimes I want him to be more sensitive.

On November 8, I finish my last Taxol treatment. It is 2:00 p.m. when Jonathan and I leave the hospital. The nurses do a funny send-off as I leave.

"We don't ever want to see you again," they say.

I feel happy for a moment that I made my goal of keeping up with the chemo and not quitting. But as we walk toward the car, deep sadness takes over me, as if I'm leaving home. For the last six months, I have had a routine and I knew the rules, and now I'm done. I don't understand why I feel the way I do. I am anxious about getting back to the real world and being normal. I am reminded of an animal kept in a cage for years and years. Their spirit becomes trapped and they can never get out of the prison even when the door opens. They see captivity as the way to be, and they can't even imagine what freedom is like. That is exactly how I feel.

6

Life after Cancer

NOVEMBER 17, 2002
Thanksgiving in Denver

My brother Jerome has invited me to spend
Thanksgiving at his home in Denver. Jerome wants to
make it a tradition, starting this year, to get everyone
together to celebrate Thanksgiving. I can see that my
cancer has had an impact on Jerome. He wants to honor
our family and not take anything for granted. It is also
time for my second three-month checkup at Mayo
Clinic. I fly to Rochester for my appointments and then
fly to Denver to spend Thanksgiving with Jerome and
the family. I feel very weak and I don't have much

energy for festivity. I have no hair, I still don't have much energy, and I'm always cold. I bring a blanket with me nearly everywhere I go (just in case), and it's very cold in Denver at this time of year. However, I very much appreciate the sentiment of his intention.

DECEMBER 16, 2002
Chemo brain

I come home from work exhausted. I look at myself in the mirror and the "me" that I see staring back is completely unrecognizable. I have gone from being skin and bones to puffy in the face, having gained 20 pounds. I am still suffering from the side effects of the steroids and chemo. I've been gaining weight, retaining fluids, and having mood swings. My skin is thinning, I'm more easily bruised, and it takes much longer to heal than it used to. My estrogen level is so low that is almost undetectable in blood tests. I am still on Prozac for hot flashes. I am very weak and have severe joint pain. My mind is foggy—the notorious "chemo brain" effect. My short-term memory is bad. I feel depressed and lethargic, as if I'm moving in slow motion.

Jonathan is still here trying to determine what to do next. He came to Florida to spend time with friends, ended up being my caregiver, and now hopes to come back into my life permanently.

I express my appreciation to Jonathan every chance I get, but I feel it's not enough. The longer he is here, the more frustrated we are both getting. I feel guilty having him here, doing so much for me. He wants us to resume our marriage, but I can't think about that part of my life. I am not healthy enough to make such a serious decision. I need more time to bounce back. I want to make that decision when I am healthy and completely recovered, but I'm not sure he understands.

There are so many obstacles in front of me right now, and the thought of trying to resolve my past issues with Jonathan overwhelms me. I remember how much I wanted to have a child when we were married and how he resisted for so long. I also remember how, when he finally agreed, it was too late. Now that I have gone through menopause, becoming a mom is not an option. That makes me even angrier. Sometimes, I feel resentful. After everything I have been going through and working full time, how can he expect *anything* from me right now?

I feel resentful that he stays home while I have to go to work, despite my condition—and then he expects me to marry him! There has never been a lack of kindness, compassion, and love between us. This is just bad timing. I am not having a good day. I feel pressured and my head starts hurting when I think about all of this. I take my anti-anxiety medication and go to bed.

DECEMBER 17, 2002
Salad bar and cancer support

I am in line at the salad bar at work when I hear a soft voice. "Are you going through chemo?" Unsure how to react, I look at her and just say yes. Then I ask her how she knew. I feel an instant connection with her. She says she went through the treatment two years ago for breast cancer and knows the look. She then says my wig just doesn't look right and my skin color gave me away. Her name is Wini. She is very smart and funny and has a high-power position at work. She invites me to attend one of her cancer support group meetings at the local hospital.

DECEMBER 18, 2002
Mom and Dad visit me at last

Mom and Dad are coming to spend Christmas with me. The thought of visiting with them brings me so much joy, even though I am still suffering severe side effects from the chemo. I have what looks like a thin covering of fuzz on my head. I'm still very bald. My skin is thin, discolored, and easily irritated. I easily get blisters on my skin. My body aches when I move. I still do not have any eyelashes. I don't seem to have any body hair anywhere. I don't have to shave my legs, and showering takes less than five minutes. I'm still worried how my parents will react when they see me.

DECEMBER 19, 2002
Magical Christmas

Jonathan is excited about Christmas, like a little child. He wants us to get a tree and decorate it together before my parents arrive. I am not in the Christmas spirit. My body is aching all over and I have no energy. I give all my energy to my job, and by the time I come home, I am completely exhausted and go directly to bed. I am fat and my mind is very foggy. It takes a lot of energy for me to do analytical work right now.

There are times, though, when I feel as if I'm gradually coming back to life and getting a breath of fresh air. Maybe this will become one of those times. I finally agree to go to the store with Jonathan to choose a tree. As soon as we come home, we put up the tree; I am excited and reinvigorated as we begin decorating it. I am surprised by my reaction. The tree looks magical, and I love it.

"This is the best-looking tree I have ever seen!" I scream with joy. The light from the glitter and the silver and yellow lights make me happy. I go to bed, and as I fall asleep, happiness permeates me for the first time in a very long while.

DECEMBER 20, 2002
Mom and Dad arrive

Mom and Dad are arriving tonight at Miami International Airport. Jonathan and I have all day to do last-minute preparations. We get the house ready for our guests, go shopping for food, and decide to buy an air mattress so that everyone will have a place to sleep. I have a guest room that Jonathan sleeps in. Now that Mom and Dad are going to be here, they will get the guest room and Jonathan will sleep on the air mattress in the living room. I worry about Mom's health. She is old, heavy, and diabetic, with high blood pressure and a heart problem. She has a hard time walking due to some foot problems.

***

We are at the airport and walk to Terminal E. I'm wearing my wig and have lots of makeup on to cover my pale face. I don't think anyone would suspect that I have been through six months of chemo. After sitting anxiously for two hours, I see Mom in a wheelchair, being pushed by one of the workers, and Dad with his big smile. I am so happy to see them. They have sat through a long flight and still don't seem tired.

Jonathan is excited about seeing my parents as well. My parents don't speak English. Since I'm fluent in both Farsi and English, I translate for them and Jonathan.

When we arrive home, it is time to get them ready for their stay.

I tell them, "It may appear that I have hair on my head, but it is not real hair. It is only a wig."

Mom turns pale. "Please don't do this to me. I can't look at your head. I will faint. My heart cannot take it."

I smile and say in a comical manner, "You don't expect me to wear this wig for a month, do you?" There is silence.

It was a long drive home from the Miami airport. It is late and we are all tired. So, we say goodnight and I go to bed. The excitement of seeing my family has exhausted me, but I am so glad that they are here.

DECEMBER 21, 2002
Making a bald appearance

The next morning, I wake up and hear noises. It sounds like everyone is up. I don't feel like putting on the wig, so I put some clothes on, walk into the kitchen, and say good morning. I had decided that it would be best for my parents to get over the shock of my bald head as soon as possible. I have little tiny hairs on my head, like when a man hasn't shaven for several days, but not as coarse.

I walk over and greet them each with a good morning kiss on the cheek. Mom is staring at my head and appears speechless. My dad grabs my hand and pulls me toward him, saying, "Bring the dome over." I laugh, and he says he wants to kiss my beautiful dome fifty times. He starts kissing and kissing my head. I lose count of the number of kisses. Jonathan is sitting at the breakfast table enjoying the attention I am getting. I feel a deep, profound love in my soul that I have never felt before.

After Dad finishes kissing my head, Mom says she wants to touch it too. Mom has always been more reserved than Dad. She has never been one for public displays of affection, and it is only in the last few years that she has started showing more physical affection to us children. She has always believed that too much affection would spoil her children. Growing up, when Dad gave me so much attention, Mom would get mad at him and ask him to stop spoiling me.

The day Mom touches my bald head is like a breakthrough day for her. The closer she gets to me, the more comfortable she is with me, but she remains skeptical and refuses to accept that I had cancer. Mom is in denial—she keeps telling me the doctors must have made a mistake. She keeps telling me, "Why you? Why should this happen to my baby? God, why didn't you give it me? Why did you give this to my baby? This is not fair."

DECEMBER 21, 2002
Bald is beautiful

My mom is feeling at home with me, and I'm happy about that. As she goes through my house, she sees more of my wigs and tells me that it is time to let them go and to throw them all away. I tell her that I spent a great deal of money on them, but she says she doesn't care. She says I don't need them. She tells me that I am as beautiful as ever, even with no hair. That is Mom's way of telling me that she loves me just the way I am.

DECEMBER 22, 2002
My big makeover day

After we throw away all the wigs, Mom wants to take me shopping at Palm Beach Garden Mall. We go to the

Saks Fifth Avenue's Chanel cosmetics counter for a makeover. The makeup artist says that he likes my look and starts to work on my face. He shows me how to do my eyes and tells me I have a unique punk rock look with my short hair. I just smile. I wonder if he knows that I just finished chemo. The shoe department is right next to the cosmetics area. While the makeup artist is doing his work, Mom waits in the shoe department, but we remain within each other's sight.

DECEMBER 31, 2002
The last day of a very challenging year

Spending time with Mom and Dad is exactly what I need right now. Today is the last day of the year, and Mom suggests we go to the beach. We sit on the sandy beach and pick up rocks. On each rock, we write our demons and what we want to release, and then throw them into the ocean. To bring us good luck, we stay by the ocean and talk to it, asking God and the universe for good health and happiness in the coming year. This is another magical day. I can't remember the last time I have been this happy.

JANUARY 2, 2003
Being touched by shingles

Today I have a new pain on my back, similar to blisters. I go to see the doctor right away, and I am told that I may be developing shingles. This is common with chemo patients. The doctor puts me on an antiviral medication right away. I am so lucky I went to the doctor promptly. Many chemo patients and elderly patients with depressed immune systems get shingles. They last for months and are very painful. Mom and Dad feel helpless, and they are very careful not to stress me or interfere with my rest. Jonathan gets my medication right away and I stay in bed most of the day.

JANUARY 6, 2003
It is a bold, bald day

Today is the first day back to work after the New Year. Per Mom's advice, I'm not wearing the wig. She keeps telling me how beautiful I am without it, and I am starting to believe her. I feel the power of Mom's words, and inside every bone and vein in my body. I put on my new makeup and wear a white shirt and tight, gray pants. My belly is sticking out in these tight pants, but I don't care. I keep hearing the voice of Mom telling me how beautiful I am. I walk proudly into my office with my chin high. I notice people's shocked faces as I walk by. This is the first time they have seen me bald.

JANUARY 18, 2003
Joining a cancer support group

My mom and dad are leaving today. My heart feels heavy. I wish I could go with them. Jonathan and I drive them to the airport and say good-bye. I feel a deep void and sadness. Will I ever see them again? I ask this question every time they leave.

***

The breast cancer support group at the local hospital is having its monthly meeting tonight. I go after work, and I see my salad bar friend, Wini. She introduces me to her friends. I am not sure what to expect from a support group. This is a completely new experience for me. I hope I do not leave the meeting more depressed than when I came in.

The meeting leader starts by announcing upcoming lectures. We then go around and introduce ourselves, each giving our backgrounds. There are women of all ages. The oldest is eighty and the youngest is thirty-two. Some have hair, some are bald and look as if they should not be there. Once they start talking, I fall in love with the group. Everyone is so open about their vulnerabilities and conditions, but at the same time, they all seem so upbeat and positive, even funny at times. There are typical women with all stages of cancer. Some are career-oriented businesswomen and some are stay-at-home moms. I feel as though I am with a group of longtime friends. They accept me right away as the new member. One of the women starts telling jokes. I find myself laughing and having a great time.

It appears that once you have faced your worst fear in life, not much else seems to matter anymore. These women are fearless. I felt an instant connection to all of them. Looking into their eyes was like saying, *I know where you have been, I have been there too, and we are all in it together.*

JANUARY 25, 2003
Art class

I decide to register in an evening art class to continue painting. When I paint, my anxiety goes away, the chattering in my head stops, and I become present and aware. I hope to have enough energy after I get home from work to go to the art class.

FEBRUARY 11, 2003
Healing dog

I talk with my neighbor Elena about how much I want a dog.

"What are you waiting for?" she says. "You know how unpredictable and fragile life can be."

Although there are years between us, I feel a strong bond with her. She is loving, respectful, and so considerate. I am self-conscious about my body right now, and she invites me to her private pool to swim. I've swum in her pool on several occasions, feeling completely at home. I call Mom and share my plan to get a little dog, and she is very encouraging as well.

I have an ad for a Maltese puppy that I took out from the *Treasure Coast* paper the other day. I call the number and arrange to meet the puppy with the owner in a local bank parking lot.

The woman pulls into the bank parking lot in a white car and introduces herself. I see an adult Maltese on her lap, which happens to be the mother of the puppy sitting on the front seat. The woman tells me that she has just moved here from Texas and is looking for a job. The puppy was born on November 15, 2002. I think, *How cool. Just a week after my last chemo and four days after my birthday.* I ask her if I can borrow the puppy for a week to see if I can handle it. She lets me take the puppy home without paying her. I never told her that I was recovering from chemo, but not much needs to be said with my bald head and pale, grayish skin.

I arrive home with this two-pound love creature. I call the owner a few hours later, and tell her that I'll keep the puppy. Now I have to come up with a name. I recall one of Jerome's last visits. While driving, he touched my bald head and started rubbing it, saying, "It looks and feels like a jelly bean." I remember how much it made me laugh. That is the first name that pops into my head. My sweet, little white Jelly Bean.

Over the next couple of weeks, word gets out in the neighborhood. Victoria stops by with a dog leash. Elena comes by to check him out and welcomes him with some doggie treats. Susana heard barking from my deck, so she walks into the backyard to check out the new addition. Everyone loves Jelly Bean and is happy for me.

Jelly Bean and I are immediately inseparable. He sleeps in my bed all night and wakes up when I do. Jonathan has house-trained him. Jelly Bean is very smart and has the most expressive eyes. He loves to sit on my shoulder and put his chin on my neck. He has given me a reason to feel happy and laugh again.

MARCH 5, 2003
Frustration with my mind and body

I feel disconnected from my physical body. My body and mind are not the same as they were before chemo. I feel damaged. My waist has completely disappeared. I have hardly any hair. My butt looks twice as big as it used to. My brain feels slow, confused, and foggy. My body movement is also awkward. Someone at work told me that my body movement is very robotic.

I avoid looking in the mirror. I remember how I used to work out and watch my diet to maintain my hourglass figure. Getting attention from the opposite sex was never a problem. I don't think men even see me anymore.

The temporary saline implants are so inflated. My skin looks so stretched and thin. My chest feels as if it is about to explode. My breasts are at least size 40 triple-D. The procedure over-expands the chest muscles in order to stretch the skin as much as possible before the final implants are put in. This is supposed to help me have natural looking breasts eventually. My weight is gradually but steadily increasing. I have constant hot flashes. I continue taking the Prozac to offset the hot flashes, and although it is helping, it has other side effects: the combination of chemo and Prozac affects my short-term memory. I find myself making stupid mistakes at work, and this concerns me. Once I sent an email and misspelled my boss's name. I felt so embarrassed, but my boss was nice and never said anything to me.

MARCH 10, 2003
Post-chemotherapy counseling

I find out that the local hospital where I had chemo provides counseling services for breast cancer patients who are going through recovery. This service is available to patients for three months, and then they send you out into the world. I decide to go see Parisa Levy, a post-chemo counselor.

I sit in the hospital waiting room and she comes toward me, greets me, and invites me into her office. She is warm and welcoming. I find her comforting, and I wonder why she is doing this work. She can't be making that much money.

She tells me she has also facilitated support groups for patients with stage IV cancer (the final stage). I talk to her about my fear, my frustration with my body, my anxiety about my future, and she listens. I also express my frustration and guilt over my situation with Jonathan. I express my anxiety about the cancer coming back and how I feel stuck in my body. She does not seem surprised by anything I tell her, as if she has heard worse. I tell her how I used to feel like a desirable woman and now I feel nothing. Her eyes get bigger as I tell her that I worked during my entire chemo treatment. She also seems surprised that Jonathan does not work. She suggests that I start practicing light yoga in the morning to help my body movement, and she gives me the name of her hairdresser in Palm Beach to style my hair, which is short but slowly growing back.

It feels so good to unload and bring everything that has been on my mind out in the open. As soon as I get home, I call the Palm Beach hairdresser for an appointment.

MARCH 15, 2003

Post-chemo side effects continue

I am still always cold and my bones are aching. My digestive system is still not working well. It takes me several days before I can digest food. I have no sense of taste. My short-term memory is still bad. Despite all this, I am happy that I am finished with chemo, and hopeful regarding my road to recovery.

Jelly Bean gives me a reason to go for walks, despite my low energy. I love holding him and communicating with him. He makes the long, dark nights more comforting. He is always there next to me. He becomes my best buddy.

I start my daily yoga practice in the morning, as Parisa suggested.

MARCH 17, 2003
Coming out

I get directions to the Palm Beach hairdresser. It takes a while, but I finally find the place. Inside, a heavyset man with an interesting mustache and beard walks toward me and puts his arms around me.

"You must be Parisa's friend."

I nod and don't share any further details. He tells me that my facial bone structure is beautiful and I have beautiful eyes. I haven't heard any such compliments for a long time. I smile on the inside. He starts cutting what little hair I have. He completely transforms my appearance. After he is done, I actual look stylish and cool, with an edge. This is much more than I expected. I get up, leave, and pay the bill. This is a lot more expensive than other haircuts I have had, but it is most definitely worth it! I begin to feel considerably better about my looks and future prospects. I'm amazed at just how much this haircut does for my self-esteem.

I am getting so much out of the counseling with Parisa. I feel free to share all my insecurities with her, and she listens and helps me with coping. She tells me that I need to connect to my body and insists I continue yoga practice daily. I compliment her on her beautiful nails. She writes down the name of the person who does hers and suggests that I make an appointment. She also wants me to look at myself in the mirror and smile, paying attention to my facial expressions and engaging in positive self-talk. She helps me set goals, something I haven't thought about in such a long time. I express my frustration with my weight and body shape, and she helps me with diet and nutrition. She tells me that the current situation with Jonathan is not helping either one of us and is keeping us both stuck. She tries to help me get my independence back, and helps me see myself as a beautiful, intelligent, and self-confident woman who has had some setbacks. She suggests that I journal daily and do deep-breathing exercises.

MAY 15, 2003

Angel everywhere

I am walking Jelly Bean when I run into Shelly, one my neighbors. Shelly is very fit and so warm and friendly. She asks me how I'm doing. I tell her how much I would like to get back into shape.

I ask her, "What do I have to do to look like you? Will you help me get back in shape?"

She smiles and says, "Absolutely!"

I never used to ask people for help so bluntly. I have always tried to do everything myself, always telling myself that I could do anything. This is a trait my mother taught me as a girl growing up in Iran. She raised me to be independent, something she could not be herself. Cancer has softened me and taught me humility. Acknowledging one's vulnerability and asking for help can be empowering. Generally, people are willing to help. I know that helping others when I am able to do so makes me feel good.

Shelly has a NordicTrack machine and brings it over right away. I thank her and try to use it the next day. Unfortunately, I am not able to keep my balance or move my arms and walk at the same time. I don't feel very coordinated, so I return it to her. We decide it's best to just go for walks. We decide to walk together every night.

The next evening at 8:30, my doorbell rings. I open the door and see Shelly with her sunshiny, beautiful smile. She asks me if I'm ready to start. We begin with a brisk walk, and just about five minutes into it, I stop to catch my breath. She keeps pushing me and pushing me to do just a little bit more. Every time I stop, she says, "How about just one more block?" I beg to go home, but then I recall that pushing myself further ultimately feels good. I return home, shower, and go straight to bed.

We walk every night for a week. I'm getting stronger, and I stop less and less often for breath. Jelly Bean and I both look forward to our nightly walk. Afterward, I come home and shower. I have been sleeping better since I started walking.

JUNE 7, 2003
Continuing with breast reconstruction surgery

I am back at the Mayo Clinic preparing for my next breast reconstruction surgery. They will be removing the temporary tissue expanders and replacing them with permanent saline implants. I am very familiar with the procedure and feel very comfortable. My surgery seems more or less routine. It takes about three hours. After I open my eyes in the recovery room, my chest feels different. I look smaller. I can't wait to look at my breasts in the mirror.

JUNE 15, 2003
Losing track of the number of surgeries I have had

Two weeks after getting the permanent implants and I'm asking myself how much more this poor body of mine can handle. I return home from Mayo exhausted and with more incisions. It will take me two to four weeks to recover. One good thing is that I now have my permanent implants. Jelly Bean is happy to see me and comes to cuddle with me in bed. Sleeping next to Jelly Bean is the best thing. I see how much he loves me. This comforts me and warms my heart. Later, I find a Milk Bone hidden under my chest—a gift from my boy. We have a special connection.

SEPTEMBER 5, 2003
Dance of Qigong

My company is offering a meditation and relaxation class every Wednesday at noon. A friend of mine suggests that I attend at least one session. I go to my first session and immediately feel better. I have heard about this particular teacher, Jon Zen, from several people, and now I have finally met him. I feel so honored. I provide him with information about my condition, and he tells me my company is doing a meditation pilot program for cancer patients. This program provides eight free sessions with Jon Zen. Jon gives me my first appointment. Jon is a ninth-degree black belt in Shaolin Kung-Fu and a Qigong master, trained in China.

It is one of the best things ever to happen to me. The weekly training I receive from Jon helps me in so many ways. He provides me with CDs that help me with breathing exercises and guided imagery to help me sleep. I notice improvement in my sleep right away. He also provides me with Qigong meditation CDs to help me start each day with breathing exercises and slow, controlled movements. I start taking long walks at night, followed by a nice shower. Then I listen to Jon's Qigong CD just before I go to bed.

Jon has a way of connecting with and speaking to the part of me that will get it. He is instrumental in my recovery from cancer's side effects. I am grateful to him. Jon introduces me to his wife, Crystal, who is an acupuncture physician. I begin acupuncture combined with Jon's Qigong sessions.

There is a shift of my energy, leading to a breakthrough. I have a deeper connection to my body and spirit. A joyous energy is with me all the time. I'm connecting with the life force. I wake up in the morning and start my day with the Qigong dance. I feel so alive. Jon uses the butterfly metaphor for my transformation. I love the comparison. He reminds me about the transformation journey from caterpillar phase, through cocoon phase, into butterfly phase ... and then into fully awakened fulfillment.

NOVEMBER 15, 2003
Jelly Bean's birthday

It is a beautiful, sunny fall day. Today is Jelly Bean's birthday. He is one year old. Jelly Bean gives me so much joy, pleasure, and happiness. I have difficulty sleeping if he isn't in bed next to me.

I am having a birthday party and inviting all my neighbors with their dogs. I have ordered a cake with his name on it. We have colorful decorations in the garage with lots of balloons. All my neighbors show up with their dogs. There are lots of toys and treats for Jelly Bean. My neighbors are delighted to see me happy and healthy.

MARCH 15, 2004
Nipple reconstruction surgery

I am back once again at the Mayo Clinic, this time for my seventh three-month oncology checkup, and to start preparing for nipple reconstruction. I was very anxious last night and was unable to sleep. I prayed while holding my crystal and practiced my Qigong breathing techniques to calm myself down.

They start with blood work and chest X-rays, followed by OB/GYN. A couple of hours later, I get the oncology test results. The news is good! I call family and close friends to share.

After the oncology checkup, I meet with the plastic surgeon for evaluation. The implants are still positioned very high; I'm not sure exactly why this is and it concerns me. The doctor tells me they'll move down gradually. Digital pictures are taken from various angles for baseline comparison. Today, the surgeons will perform my nipple reconstruction surgery. I never imagined it would take so much effort to recreate what God had given me; they will be using implants for the nipples and will place small cups over my breasts to avoid any pressure on the nipples while they heal. I have to wear the cups for the next ten days.

JUNE 1, 2004
Jonathan goes to his mother's farm

I am getting stronger and need Jonathan's help less and less. He is trying to find a purpose for himself. His mom is having some medical problems, so he decides to go to her farm in the Midwest to take care of her.

SEPTEMBER 5, 2004

Life goes on ... Mom has a stroke

On my way to the Mayo Clinic for checkup number eight, I receive a call from my sister Francesca telling me that Mom has had a stroke. Francesca is in the hospital with her. I feel numb after the call, and try to call Mom at the hospital, but they say she is unable to speak. I am not thinking about myself anymore, and I am more concerned about her. I heard that she was having headaches when they took her to the ER, where they gave her medication to reduce her blood pressure. I'm told that it's possible the medication may have caused her stroke, although she has not been in good health for as long as I can remember.

I call Mom at the hospital a little later and I am able to speak with her. She can barely talk. Her speech is slurred and she tells me that she is very tired. I try to encourage her, but she tells me that they are killing her in the hospital, and she wants me to come home to be with her and help her. I feel so helpless thinking about my mother being so sick in the hospital in Iran and so far away from me. I want to scream loud and blame someone for all of this. Why does this have to happen to our family? Is this how it is all supposed to end? I find myself gazing at the Mayo garden, reminded of when I was sick and all alone.

Growing up in Iran, I was always the one helping my mother and taking her to the doctor. I quickly begin to plan my trip to be with my mom in Tehran.

***

It is a very long flight to Tehran from Miami. By the time I arrive at the airport, it is nearly twenty-four hours later due to all the layovers. I'm exhausted. I see my dad waving at me. It is so nice to see him. He puts his big arms around me and gives me a hug. I feel comforted.

We drive from the airport to their condo but don't say much in the car. It's a forty-five-minute ride. We arrive at the condo and I go to Mom's room right away. Her hair is shorter than when I last saw her. She's sitting up on the bed waiting for me to come home to her. She smiles as I walk in. I give her a kiss. She does not say much. Dad has hired a live-in nurse to sleep in the same room with her. I thank the nurse for being with Mom and give her some European chocolate. My Dad seems reassured that I'm finally home. I give Mom a goodnight kiss and go to the guest room to sleep.

The next day, I organize all of Mom's medications, create a daily routine for her, and help her get ready for breakfast. I plan all of her meals. We contact the physical therapist to work on her recovery. I am maintaining a positive attitude and also want my mom to believe that she will walk again. I know that a good attitude has a positive impact on health and assists in recovery from illness. Also, having support from someone who can help with organization and structure is very comforting during an illness. Dad has empowered me to do whatever I need to do to help Mom. I am so glad to be here.

Mom is unable to sleep at night. I stay up with her until she falls asleep, which is usually during the early morning hours. She has nightmares every night, and wakes up frightened and wondering where she is. One night, while awake, she talks to her sister, who passed away many years ago. Another night, she tells me she is in a graveyard looking for her father. I assume it is due to the medications she has been prescribed. Her physical therapy has finally started, and she does not like it; however, I won't let her quit. I have become my mom's mom.

Having gone through my own illness and recovery has given me so much strength and a voice that sometimes surprises even me. That voice speaks to my mother and helps her see the possibility of not giving up. I know what my mother is made of, and won't let her forget it. I am her courage. I see this as a temporary setback.

Eventually, she begins making progress; it is a good sign. When we help her, she is able to stand up and walk a few steps. It's very painful for her to bathe; I'm very concerned that she'll fall and break a hip. She is tired of staying home, but we're not sure where we can take her in this condition. I play music for her. I show her pictures of all of us as kids, and I ask questions to make sure she is still able to recognize everyone. I make sure the nurses are doing their job at all times. I eventually have to replace two of the nurses due to neglect.

OCTOBER 26, 2004

Mom will never walk again

Mom appears to be in very good spirits today; we are all attending to her needs and she seems happy. I'm putting my energy into helping her walk again. Dad is concerned about me since he doesn't want me to get sick too.

Visitors have been coming to see us every night. When they arrive, we help Mom into a wheelchair and take her to the living room. Last night, we had a lot of company for dinner, so we ordered food from a local restaurant—one of Mom's favorites. Francesca's daughter, Ladie, drew a picture of all of us, including one of Mom with a red blanket on her lap.

Today, after fourteen years, my sister heard from US immigration. She is finally able to move to the United States with the rest of her siblings. This has always been Mom's biggest dream for Francesca, but I cannot believe the timing. Why couldn't this have happened a year ago, when Mom was in better health? Still, I am happy for the good news. We try to explain it to Mom. We aren't quite sure whether she understands.

Mom slept very well last night. We are hopeful that she will be able to walk on her own soon. I go to Mom's room to meet up with the nurse, and we get Mom freshened up for breakfast. She doesn't seem hungry, and her physical therapist is here. I leave her room, so that the physical therapist can start.

It is about 10:00 a.m. when I go to the living room. I sit listening to opera as I look out the front window at the panoramic view of Tehran's beautiful mountains. I take out sketch paper and a pencil and start drawing, inspired by the Zagros Mountains. Once again, art comes to my rescue as it did during the darkest days of my illness; I lose myself in the beauty before me, as I continue to take in the view.

A short while later, the physical therapist calls me to Mom's room. I walk in and she says, "Your mom is not cooperating again." Sometimes, Mom does that to avoid doing the exercises, and we have to talk her into it.

"Mom," I say, "please help us out here. We want you to get well as soon as possible."

She looks straight ahead, her eyes glistening, as though mesmerized by some vision. She doesn't say a word. I call my brother David and ask him to talk to

Mom. As soon as I put the phone to Mom's ear, she says, "Hi," then falls backward. Her face goes immediately from golden pink to blue gray, and she looks as if she has no control over her ability to speak. Thinking she might swallow her tongue and unsure what to do, I panic. I give her mouth-to-mouth resuscitation, but she doesn't respond. I call for an ambulance, and while waiting, we try to revive her. I am the only family member in the room with the physical therapist, the nurse, and our longtime family friend.

The ambulance doesn't arrive until two hours later. Dad finally comes home, enters the room, and asks me to leave. Five minutes later, the nurse comes out and tells me that Mom is gone. Dad comes out and walks toward me. We look at each other with disbelief and sadness; he hugs me and we both start crying aloud, holding each other.

My Dad asks, "How am I going to tell my children they have lost their mother?"

We hold each other for the longest time, with tears in our eyes.

OCTOBER 28, 2004
Sharing light

Today is my mom's funeral, and many guests attend the ceremony. Unfortunately, my two younger brothers who live in the United States were not able to come. My mother's body, wrapped in a white sheet, is placed inside the grave that was prepared the night before in a well-known cemetery called Behesht Zahra. I go inside and lean over to give Mom a last hug. My meditation crystals are in my pocket, and I break the thread holding the crystals together, remove one, and place it next to Mom. These crystals have helped me see light during some of my darkest moments; I hope that this crystal does the same for Mom. I recall the night I dreamt about Glow, the rainbow that was lost in the dark. I ask Glow to be with Mom and show her there is nothing to fear. I'm sure that Mom will find her way home, and we will be together again one day.

NOVEMBER 7, 2004
Return to the United States

It's a longer flight home than it was to Tehran to be with my Mom. I have lots of time to reflect on what has happened. I'm heartbroken that Mom is gone. When I was a child, Mom used to tell me that when she died, she wanted me to be with her. I'm happy that I was able to be there for her, but am so sad at the same time.

On my flight, I find myself sitting next to a preacher. I tell him about my experience and my mom's death. He says that I should feel blessed because God chose me to be there with her during that time. His words comfort me.

After I return home, Jonathan and I spend time discussing the future. He has become restless staying at home every day. He sees me feeling healthier and needing him less and less. He looks for a reason to stay; he is semi-retired and wants to settle down with me. Planning for the future is not even on my horizon. I feel like I am just coming back from hell, and on top of that I'm grieving my mother's passing. I'm only able to think as far into the future as my next oncology checkup.

The mere fact that I'm having this conversation with Jonathan just stresses me out more. Cancer has changed my identity and how I look at myself. I need to build myself again from the ground up. I am drowned in grief from the loss of my mother and still recovering from the side effects and the impact of multiple surgeries and six months of aggressive chemotherapy.

We care for each other very much and have an unbreakable bond. We both know that we'll be true friends for life, but right now I can't see us being married again. Jonathan feels that his life now has more meaning, having helped me through a life-threatening illness. We each feel that there was a bigger reason for our being in each other's life. I tell him that I have forgiven him for not being supportive during our marriage when I needed him the most and wanted to have children. He says he very much regrets not having children with me, but now chemo has robbed me of that opportunity. We hug each other and say good-bye.

AUGUST 1, 2005
Changing jobs

I am bored with my job. I feel that my boss does not want to give me any challenging projects; perhaps it is because he does not want me to be stressed out, but I feel as though I am ready for a challenge. I don't want to be treated like a cancer patient for the rest of my life. I want to be treated normally. I don't want to be defined by my cancer.

For the last two years, I haven't spent much time thinking about my career, and now that I'm feeling so much better, I begin to consider a different position in my company. One of the advantages of working for a large company is the number of opportunities that are available.

SEPTEMBER 1, 2005
Getting involved with the Komen Foundation

I want to start volunteering again. For many years, I have participated in Komen's Race for the Cure, running the 5K with friends, celebrating life, and cheering for all the survivors. The Komen Foundation is always seeking volunteers to raise money for the cause; I want to give something back for all the support the foundation has given me, so I begin fundraising for them.

OCTOBER 15, 2005
Going back to Iran

It's been almost a year since I lost my mother. It is our family tradition to have a memorial ceremony on the one-year anniversary of a family member's passing; honoring this tradition will be especially important to me on my mother's one-year anniversary. I fly to Tehran to be with my family for the anniversary reception. We are expecting more than two hundred guests for dinner.

The club where we are having the ceremony is very elegant. When I walk in, the decorations are strikingly beautiful; the only clue that this is a funeral anniversary is the black ribbon wrapped around white roses on each table. The white roses are a symbol of my mother. One night last year, while I was taking care of her, she could not sleep and I was trying to comfort her.

I asked, "What is your favorite flower?"

She answered, "Roses."

"What color?"

"White" was her reply.

I keep hearing Mom's voice in my head, lecturing me about how I need to go out and have more fun. She used to complain to me that my life was too mechanical; she always encouraged me to meet more people and start dating.

I now feel strong and ready to begin seeing people. I begin to open myself to the possibility of new relationships.

NOVEMBER 5, 2005
Back to normal life

I'm back home in Florida now and settling into my normal routines. Shelly and I go for walks two to three nights a week. She is concerned about me being alone all the time. She thinks I should open up to meet new people and form new relationships. I feel very insecure about starting a new relationship. Shelly gives me suggestions about makeup and clothes; she helps me build my self-confidence. I don't feel good about my body. I'm still twenty pounds overweight, which concerns me. I have been in survival mode for such a long time.

NOVEMBER 17, 2005
Making a new connection

One day, during a meeting for a local fundraising project, I meet William. He recently moved to Florida from Vermont to be close to his elderly parents. He is polite and seems nice and sincere. He has dark, intense eyes, and when he looks at me, I feel that he sees into my soul. I enjoy the attention. We decide to meet for dinner one night after work at a local restaurant. What should I wear? I don't know, since I haven't been out on a date in such a long time. I feel the need to hide the excess 20 pounds somehow. I want to look attractive. William is very slender and I am anxious about how much fatter I've gotten and how I will look standing next to him. I'm not sure why I feel that I have to justify myself. I wonder whether I should talk about my breast cancer right away.

William appears to be in very good physical condition. He has a pleasant personality and, from what I can see, he maintains a healthful lifestyle. I decide casual is good, so I put on jeans with a simple top, then drive to the restaurant to meet him. We sit down, order drinks, and begin conversing.

He is a great listener, and I like to talk. He seems very interested in what I have to say. I tell him that I'm a breast cancer survivor. I can tell he is not sure how to react to that. It is an awkward moment; however, I prefer to get it out in the open and discuss it. I need to know right away if he has any reservations about this before I invest too much time and effort in exploring a relationship.

Having not been on a date for years, this feels so strange to me; I haven't seen myself in this light for such a long time. I ask myself if I am viewed as attractive and desirable. It wasn't too long ago when my body felt mutilated with one surgery after another.

***

William and I start spending more time together. I am happy with the pace of the relationship. He takes me out to see a ballet, *The Nutcracker Suite,* and invites me to a New Year's Day luncheon party at his place. I enjoy meeting his parents, although I am finding it hard to be "normal." I try to act normal and talk about normal things, but I feel like a fake, pretending to be like everyone else. Still, I am happy that William and I are becoming friends.

JANUARY 7, 2006
It is a good life

Life seems to be progressing normally for a change. I was able to find a new position in my company that is challenging and interesting. William and I both welcome our friendship. I have no expectations from William. He is a good influence on me. He encourages me to start working out.

William and I have many differences. He is a typical engineer, disciplined and organized. He thrives on routine, and I am just the opposite. He is very quiet, while I am more lively and outspoken, although he seems drawn to my spiritual and creative energy. Despite our differences, we are developing a fondness toward each other. William invites me to the rowing club to watch him row; I have never seen anyone row before, and I prepare myself to meet some of his rowing friends. I watch him row and see a couple of dolphins playing in the distance. I fall in love with the beauty and the art of rowing.

I want to share more about my fight with breast cancer and how it has changed me. I offer to show William the photos of my journey, but he seems reluctant and uncomfortable. I decide that he isn't ready for this and change my mind.

William and I are planning to go to rowing camp in Vermont in two months. I have to brush up on my swimming skills in case the rowing shell turns over and I end up in the water. I arrange for private swimming lessons. Everything William and I do together revolves around sports or food. William's kitchen is incredibly well-organized, and I feel a little intimidated. One day, I opened a kitchen drawer and every single Tupperware container had a lid on it; I was very impressed.

It's March, and once again, I'm due at the Mayo Clinic for my annual checkup. William drops me off at the airport and wishes me luck. I'm on my own now.

After I return home, I begin taking swimming lessons. My swimming instructor meets me at my community pool each Saturday, helping me to improve my technique by having me swim laps and work on breathing. Swimming is fun but challenging, since I have a fear of deep water that I have been trying to overcome.

In May, William and I travel to the Craftsbury Sculling Camp in Vermont for training. The instructors are world gold-medal-winning athletes. Everyone seems to be in absolutely perfect physical condition, and I'm feeling very self-conscious. We row three times a day, but my implants are making it awkward for me. I don't want anyone to know about my implants and the cancer, because I want to be treated just like everyone else. I am the least natural and obviously the most challenged student. Fortunately, I don't get any pity from the instructor.

Despite all the physical and emotional challenges, I'm having the best time of my life at rowing camp. It is like being a teenager again, playing all day long.

It's the last day of camp and we have a race. I finish last, but that I am proud of myself. I'm still in the game! I've completed the week and feel proud of myself that I stuck it out to the end.

I've also gone sailing with William twice. He owns a beautiful sailboat and has been trying to teach me how to sail. I feel clumsy and out of balance on the sailboat. One day, trying to get off the sailboat, I hit my forehead on the rail, fell backward, and ended up in the water. It was a close call that could have been disastrous. I ended up with cuts and bruises. I've had mixed feelings about sailing since.

JULY 1, 2006
Chemo side effects

It's been four years and I still have residual effects from the chemo treatments. My short-term memory isn't as good as it used to be. I am not able to multitask as well as I used to. I have residual bone and joint pain, and I tire very easily. When I share my frustrations with William, he doesn't seem able to empathize with me.

Today, I learn about another change in my immune system as an aftereffect of the chemo. After I return from rowing, I accidentally step on a red fire-ant hill in the grass. I don't even realize it. Within fifteen minutes, I am getting a rash and am beginning to itch all over. I don't know what is going on. I lie on the ground. I feel burning inside, as though my organs are on fire. I still have no idea what is happening. I get up but am extremely uncomfortable. We leave to go to get breakfast, and while sitting and eating, my tongue begins to swell. I ask William to take me to the ER, recalling that it is common to develop allergic reactions following chemo treatments. After that incident, I now carry an EpiPen with me.

I'm on my way back to the Mayo Clinic for my fifth annual checkup. By now, I can make this trip with my eyes closed. William drops me off at the airport and wishes me luck. I wonder how he feels about my body and my going for a checkup all alone. I wonder if he would like to accompany me, but I am afraid to ask. Communication seems challenging at times; he never seems able to share his feelings. Still, I'm very grateful that he has agreed to take care of Jelly Bean while I am away.

7

Five Years
Cancer-Free

OCTOBER 2007–OCTOBER 2011

My most recent checkup marks my five-year anniversary of being cancer-free. This is an important milestone in the life of a breast cancer survivor. I call all my friends and family to give them the good news. Elizabeth comes from Santa Fe to spend a week celebrating with me.

I go to the Mayo Clinic for another plastic surgery. I have been having a considerable amount of discomfort with the saline implants. The implants aren't moving downward as they should, and there is still excess skin that needs to be removed.

When I told William about the surgery, I downplayed it, telling him that it was minor, Now that I'm here, I see that it's much more complicated than I expected. I feel isolated and alone in my hotel room while I recover. I don't feel comfortable sharing any of this with William. He rarely asks questions about my cancer, and I continually recall the time I wanted to share my cancer recovery photos and he seemed uncomfortable.

Still, with William's help and friendship, I've learned to embrace and enjoy the Florida lifestyle and am working on getting back in shape. I have always loved running, and exercise in general, but I would never have imagined that I'd get into rowing and swimming—not to mention trying to sail! William and I enjoy each other's company, but neither of us is able to dream about or discuss a future together. My heart longs for depth and intimacy in a relationship.

When I return home, William and I acknowledge that we have reached a plateau in the relationship—we're not moving forward—so we decide to go our separate ways. Despite our best intentions, it is still painful at this juncture, the end of our familiar and comfortable, yet incomplete relationship.

Jon Zen helps me grow and question what I should learn from the experience. I begin to question and better understand what I truly want, need, and deserve in a relationship now. I've never given this much thought to the subject before. Still, I find myself in the familiar territory of being all alone, and I wonder if I will ever meet my soul mate.

Meanwhile, the challenges of day-to-day life continue. It is time to arrange for my annual checkup. I'm reminded of my number-one priority: my health. Everything else moves to the back of the line!

8

Ten Years
Cancer-Free

OCTOBER 2012

It has been ten years since my last chemo treatment. During my last checkup, my plastic surgeon informed me that they may need to replace my breast implants. I am developing a condition known as "bottoming out." This is caused by weakening of the tissue at the bottom of the breasts and the weight of the implants forcing them to move sideways instead of downward. There is a new surgical technique available, using AlloDerm. AlloDerm is a tissue matrix originally used for burn victims. Created from donated human skin, it is placed on the human tissues, where it provides new tissue regeneration. Blood flows into the preserved vascular channels in the AlloDerm, literally becoming part of the human body. I will plan for this surgery when I go back to Mayo for my next annual checkup.

***

I recently reconnected with Leo, an old friend from twenty years ago when I lived in the Midwest. He is planning to drive to Key West to visit his sister, and asks if we can meet for dinner when he passes through. Although we have kept in touch sporadically, I have not seen him in twenty years; now he's driving to my house to pick me up for dinner. It is like traveling back in time. As soon he walks in, the old chemistry between us is back.

Leo and I have so much to share after twenty years. He is coming back down to Florida this year for Christmas and New Year's. His goal is to move to Florida in six months or so. Meanwhile, I am nervous and conflicted about getting involved in a long-distance relationship.

With Leo, I change my outlook toward what is possible in a relationship. I feel optimistic and hopeful, seeing many possibilities. After he returns to his home in the Midwest, we talk for hours on the phone and there is a deep sense of connection. This feels so new and refreshing.

One afternoon, when he was in town, we were watching the 1954 romantic comedy *Sabrina*, with Audrey Hepburn and Humphrey Bogart. I shared with Leo how I always dreamt of falling in love and going to Paris. I wondered, *Will we ever go to Paris together?*

Leo and I continue to get to know each other despite the long-distance challenge. I talk to Leo about my upcoming breast surgery, and he insists on going with me. I'm not sure what to think of that. On the one hand, I am flattered that he wants to go with me, and on the other hand, I want to go alone. I don't understand myself. Over the years, I have gotten used to going to Mayo by myself. It has become my sanctuary and the source of my spiritual growth. He doesn't understand why I don't want him to go. I finally understand how important it is for him to be there, and I agree that he can accompany me.

Leo meets me at the Rochester Methodist Hospital at Mayo Clinic for my surgery. He appears calm and is very attentive. The nurse comes to take me to the operating room. I recognize her and am happy to see a familiar face.

After being prepped and taken into surgery, the last thing I remember is that I was freezing cold. When I open my eyes, I'm told that the surgery took longer than expected and that I almost stopped breathing. This is the first time that has happened, but for some reason, it didn't scare me. I feel that the energy of the divine was with me. I look at Leo and he looks drained and unsure what to think. I wonder if he regrets being here. I wonder if it was too soon in our relationship to share this much. I close my eyes as the pain medication takes its effect.

Recovering from surgery is a challenge, but I've done it so many times that I am becoming good at it. Sharing this experience with Leo feels awkward. I find myself thinking back to when I first had my double mastectomy and Jonathan was there with me. I realize that my comfort level just isn't the same with Leo as it was with Jonathan. I don't yet feel comfortable sharing such a personal experience with him. As I recover from surgery, Leo tries to help, and I'm suddenly feeling self-conscious. I don't feel like being around anyone, but I restrain myself and try to be civil. I am not good company when I am in such severe pain, and the side effects of the drugs are just making things worse. The medication is making me drowsy and moody.

When I am back in Florida, Leo takes another week off of work and comes to help me with recovery. He is able to work remotely. I spend most of the time in bed, recovering from the pain of the surgery and experiencing a new normal with Leo. The week goes by very quickly, and Leo returns home.

***

Two weeks after my surgery, it is early morning. I open my eyes to the first light of day. I'd dreamt of rowing in the river, seeing the sunrise, and watching baby dolphins play in the water.

Now, I find myself stuck to my bed, barely able to move. I had a horrible night, not falling asleep until sometime after 3:00 a.m., overwhelmed and worrying about not healing fast enough. I wonder if this is all worth it. I am in such a dark place, feeling alone, and wondering how I've made it this far.

I feel restless and stuck in my damaged, pained, fragile body. My mind feels so strange that it's disconcerting. I remind myself that all the medications are making me depressed, confused, and foggy—not to mention moody. I am wearing a compression bra with adhesive silicone pads to keep my breasts intact, with all the incisions and stitches. I feel so squeezed that I can hardly breathe. I am not able to move much in my bed. I have pillows under my right and left arms. I have three pillows slanted beneath my back and two more under my knees to help with blood circulation. The nausea and constipation caused by the pain medicine is making me miserable. I have been slowly eating saltine crackers, one small bite at a time.

It is just me and Jelly Bean here now. Considering the five-pound weight restriction imposed on me, it takes some maneuvering to get Jelly Bean on the bed at night. He is up every morning at 6:00 a.m., staring into my eyes, waiting for me to get up and take him for a walk. It takes me a long time and a lot of effort just to get out of bed. But I am determined to get out and spend time in the fresh air. I am reminded of what my dad always tells me: "Look to nature for answers to life's mysteries." I hear this voice in my head telling me to get out of the house and go for a walk. The pain and discomfort in my chest are agonizing, but I finally get us both out of bed.

Stepping outside, we find it is a beautiful fall day. Even though it is uncomfortable with all the new incisions, I try to take in several deep breaths. Upon returning from our walk, I open all the shades to let the sun in, and take in its warmth and energy. I start the kettle for tea and even walk to my bedroom to organize the bed. It's too painful to make it, but I can at least rearrange the pillows and make it a bit neater and more inviting. As I drink my tea, I hear my beloved Jelly Bean munching on his food. Rays of sunlight shine through the window. I smile.

I'm feeling especially disconnected from my body and have gained twelve more pounds following surgery. I'm still not allowed to row. I hate the way I look and feel. Old, familiar feelings are coming back. I'm feeling very unattractive and losing my self-confidence. Looking at my twenty-four-inch incisions in the mirror, I wonder if I still look sexy; I certainly don't feel that I do. I need reassurance that I'm still wanted, desired, attractive, and loved.

When I receive the bill from Mayo for my surgery, I gasp for breath. My insurance pays 80 percent and I'm responsible for the remaining 20 percent. I arrange to make monthly installments with the Mayo Clinic business office, so I can pay it off by the end of the year, even though the amount I owe is astoundingly high.

Going back to work is shock to my system. As soon as I walk in, my boss asks how I am and proceeds to hand me a critical assignment, saying, "I feel guilty about giving this to you, but the work has to get done." I am back in survival mode—stressing over work, the commute, life. It seems like a never-ending cycle.

***

After every surgery, after every knife that cuts me open, *I lose myself and my connection to my core and have to learn to love myself all over again.* Following surgery, it takes months for the body to eliminate the residual effects of the anesthesia. What's more, my acupuncture physician tells me that the heart remembers the trauma from the surgery and takes months to heal. That's when I feel as though something is missing inside. *I feel disconnected with myself, and it starts to affect my relationship with the outside world. When I feel less than whole, I look elsewhere for something to fill the void.* In the past when I have done this, I expected my partner to fill that void and make me feel complete. After each surgery, I start over at zero, at the beginning, and have to struggle back to where I feel complete and whole again. I am just beginning to return to my old self.

My friend Samantha always tells me that you need to experience all four seasons when you are in a relationship with someone. After the surgery, my relationship with Leo is not the same. We maintain our routine evening phone conversation for a while, but eventually it becomes stale and repetitive, and we have difficulty reaching any depth. I feel a lack of independence and freedom of self-expression, and I think he feels trapped and obligated to stay in touch. We both realize the long-distance relationship is too stressful and decide it is best to move on.

After it's over, I realize how much I had opened my heart, and I feel disappointed and vulnerable. I struggle with closure initially, but I am finally able to make peace with it.

I ask Jon what the lesson is here. He tells me that I was paying attention, unlike before, where I was sleep-walking in my relationships.

I go back to art to pamper my soul. Renee knows how much I like painting, and she knows I work full time and cannot take her daytime workshops during the week. She offers a monthly Saturday art workshop so I can attend.

One day, I share my dream to go to Paris with Renea. Europe is a second home to Renea, as she lived there many years. She smiles and says, "To avoid setting yourself up for failure, you need to just forget your dream and just go. We will be going to Paris soon, so start working on your French."

9

What I Have Learned So Far

Before my encounter with cancer, I never knew how much strength I had in me. My idea of what life is has been altered forever. I have gone through about ten surgeries and more than seventy checkups. I counted the number of times needles have been poked in my arms and the total was more than 500.

There is a force bigger than all of us—God, divine spirit, energy, or whatever your religion or spiritual practice may call it. To talk to this source, I surrender and accept what is, and let the divine inside of me begin a conversation with the divine of the universe. My strength comes from connecting to this source of power.

I surround myself with positive people who have earned my trust and with whom I can be vulnerable yet still feel safe. The medical procedures that I've survived over the years have been a test of my relationships with family, friends, and complete strangers. It is easy to have friends when you are at the top of your game; but my true friends are still with me after all this time and have stuck with me when things were most difficult. *I've learned that I do not have control over what happens in life.* I can always do my best and hope for the best outcome, however. I've learned how insignificant I am in this universe, and as a result, have stopped taking myself so seriously. I know that I am nothing by myself. *Real power comes from my heart and my ability to connect with, move, and inspire others. It cannot be taken away.* I feel blessed to have strong connections to my friends, family, and other caring people who just seem to "show up" in my life at the right time and in the right place.

I've discovered comfort in simple things. The pleasure of walking outside after a rain shower, rowing at dawn and seeing the stars, having the first cup of coffee in the morning while watching the sunrise, chocolate, hot tea in the afternoon, and lots of time with Jelly Bean—these things bring light to my life.

When my body is not healthy, my mind is not healthy. For this reason, I work out three to four times each week and row any chance I get. I eat healthful food most of the time. I stay away from fast food and eat plenty of fruit, vegetables, and nuts.

Through my art, I process and purge my unwanted negative energy and bring peace into my heart and life. The language of art is similar to the language of love. Art helps heal my wounds and brings me to a place of joy and inspiration. When I feel disconnected and lonesome, I seek refuge in art. I paint, and the loneliness fades away. I have created three new paintings so far this year.

Jon Zen, my transformational coach and spiritual advisor, continues guiding me in my search for enlightenment. *I am moving on with my life, do my best to live in the present moment at all times, and accept my life for what it is. As a result, life gets better and better every day.* I don't think about the past too much. When I live in the present, I enjoy life more, just as it is. I bring to life what

I need the most by looking inward; to seek externally what is missing inside is a futile exercise.

I have learned that all feelings are temporary and it is best not to get too attached to any of them. No matter how happy I am or how terrible life may seem at any given moment, it will change. As my Zen master reminds me often, "Be the sky, not the cloud." Clouds come and go in various directions and have varying degrees of grayness, but they are not permanent. I have learned there is always a lesson to learn when we are faced with failure in life. We just may not always be ready to learn the lesson.

When new people walk into my life, I don't expect them to be open and loving toward me just because of all I have been through. I've learned to give them as much time as they need to put their arms around my experience. They may never grasp the extent of the challenges and changes, both physical and emotional, that I've had to go through. I don't get upset and disappointed anymore when others are not where I am in their understanding. Their willingness to try to understand is a good start. Faith, health, friends, family, my pet, and giving something back in this lifetime are my priorities.

I don't let cancer define me, but I can't deny the profound impact it has had on me. I have learned that one of the easiest ways to feel happy is to be generous and give something of myself to those in need. Love is the only thing that matters in this lifetime. The times I felt unloved and wanted to be loved were the times the universe shook my world, woke me up, and taught me that true love starts with self-love. I have struggled at times to love myself through all the obstacles. But I now know it is a mistake to fall into the trap of thinking a new relationship will fill the emptiness.

I've learned to pay attention when true love comes into my life. Love is like a butterfly that comes and visits unexpectedly. It is a waste of time to chase it; it will have to find us in its own time. I have also learned that is okay to walk away from a relationship when it is not right.

The more I pay attention to my surroundings and to others, the less I worry about myself. It has been more than ten years since I found that I had cancer, and now I'm healthy and happy. For me, cancer was not a death sentence but a wakeup call. I've learned to embrace spirituality; a healthful lifestyle of diet, exercise, and

184 | ERIN ARBABHA

timely checkups; a sense of humor; and a routine of giving back, and constantly learning and surrounding myself with positive people. I don't have as much anxiety or worry as I used to. I accept that life is temporary and something to be treasured. I constantly strive to make the best of my life and do my best to live a life with no regrets. And I remember just how lucky I am to really live in paradise.

What Patients Can Know and Do

Get a second opinion no matter who the doctor is; confident doctors will even encourage you to do it.

Pamper yourself.

Get yourself a fluffy blanket and a stuffed animal that you can sleep with.

Get rid of clutter in your bedroom. Make it very light and colorful.

Get a foot massage.

Create a sanctuary in the bedroom, with the right light and comfortable, clean sheets and pillows.

Surround yourself with beauty and art.

Listen to inspirational and relaxing music, and make it easily accessible in your bedroom.

Take an art class.

Make sure you have the right clothes for after the surgery.

Take a warm bath when you are cold.

Have an electric heating pad by your bed.

Never underestimate the power of ice cream.

Take yoga.

Do Qigong.

Dance, even if you have incisions or scars and see no reason to dance.

Try acupuncture to eliminate the side effects of chemo.

Remind yourself that no matter how bad you are feeling at the time, it is only temporary. You'll get through it.

Write everything down in your planner. Include milestones regarding your treatment, such as your first chemo, when you expect to lose your hair, when you expect to be weak, when you expect to be susceptible to infection, etc. Chemo makes you forgetful and irritable and makes it difficult to concentrate.

Write everything down that you want to do.

Appreciate the fact that you will not be able to raise your arm for at least a month, or more, depending on the severity of your surgery.

Discuss the possibility of freezing your eggs before chemo. This was not an option when I had chemo. (Chemo can put you into early menopause.)

Join a support group.

Set goals and milestones for your progress.

Try to keep a normal schedule as much as possible. Some routine and structure are comforting.

Write letters to friends who mean a great deal to you.

Spend time with nature. It is very comforting to know that the earth, the sun, the moon, and the stars are still here with you.

Maintain normal social activity. Don't disconnect yourself from the world completely. Start a blog and share what you are going through. Your experiences can help others more than you know.

Participate in fund-raising activities for the cause. There is always someone else who needs more help than you do. Helping is healing.

Pay attention to the medical staff. If you feel uncomfortable with the approach of a doctor or nurse, ask for another one.

Always make a list of questions and concerns before you go and see your doctor.

Get a second opinion, away from the local network of doctors in your community. Sometimes, doctors feel obligated to one another and won't disagree with the diagnoses of their colleagues, especially if they happen to be reputable, prominent community members.

Once you lose your hair, you will get cold easily, so buy yourself a comfortable cap and blanket to carry with you.

Always have your art supplies handy.

Keep a notebook or laptop handy so that you can write.

Have audio books available to listen to when you are too weak to leave your bed.

Always have some ginger or cinnamon candy or saltine crackers with you, to defeat nausea.

Change your closet. Reinvent yourself.

Open your eyes and mind. Pay attention to what is around you.

Breathe deeply.

Keep a record of all insurance correspondence in writing.

Do daily affirmations.

Stay away from crowded and noisy places; they can drain your energy and may affect your immune system.

Have light colors around you, especially yellow, pink, soft orange, and light green. These colors always made me feel good.

Prepare for downtime and celebrate good times.

Take it one day at a time.

Be here now.

Set goals and reward yourself after the completion of each chemo.

Follow all the holiday celebrations, such as Halloween, Thanksgiving, and Christmas, and participate even if you don't feel like it.

Get a pet.

Stay positive.

Accept your situation, move on, and deal with it.

Cry or scream if you need to.

Do expect miracles.

Watch your senses as they go away and as they come back. Some of your senses may be weakened because of chemo. For example, your senses of taste, smell, touch, and sometimes vision may be impaired.

Remind yourself that you are more than your mind and what your mind may be telling you.

Don't try to hang on to the old person that you were. You will not be the same person after this is over.

Don't waste your energy on people who are not your friends.

Don't put your life on hold just because you have cancer.

Don't ever say, "Why me?"

Don't expect too much from yourself.

Don't worry about the cancer coming back. It is outside of your control. Worrying is just going to make you feel worse. Distract yourself by taking up a hobby or being with friends, and be in the moment.

Don't expect sympathy from others.

Don't expect your body to ever be the same.

Don't dwell on what you should have done.

Don't give up hope, no matter what.

During chemo, don't cook anything that has a strong smell, such as garlic, onions, or liver.

Don't eat your favorite foods after chemo. This leaves a long-lasting negative effect in your mind. To this day, I cannot eat lasagna due to vomiting it up after one of my chemo sessions. The foods that worked best for me while I was going through this were mashed potatoes, rice, Jell-O, watermelon, and chocolate milkshakes.

Don't hold back tears. You will need to go through a grieving process.

What Caregivers Can Know and Do

Honor my dignity. There may be times I can't control it and may have to throw up in unexpected places. A scent or odor can trigger this and make me nauseated.

Celebrate with me.

Encourage me.

Inspire me.

Love me.

Protect me.

Let me sleep.

Plan get-togethers around my energy level.

If I am angry and depressed, don't lecture me. Just give me some space. My body is going through a lot.

Let me know how much you want to be here with me, because I may feel guilty.

Let me grieve, but don't leave me alone.

Work around my mood. Don't take my outbursts personally. The medication, especially the chemo and painkillers, have side effects that cause mood swings, including unintentional anger.

Take me out for short walks, even if it is only for five minutes.

Create a routine around my treatments. For example, always go to the beach on day three or always go out to dinner on day seven after chemo, or help me to take a bath.

Night times are tough for me; keep checking on me and give me positive words of encouragement.

Put your hand on my heart and send me positive energy.

Pray for me.

I'm going through a lot. My body and spirit are being challenged. I have no energy. Listen to me and offer to help. Be ready to help.

Rub my feet.

Feel my body and give me some of your energy.

Meditate with me.

Hold me, hug me, and remind me of the sunshine.

Educate yourself about cancer and chemotherapy.

Always have the ingredients for chicken soup handy.

Disinfect the environment and always have antibacterial cleaning solution around.

Don't take anything I say or do personally. I just feel miserable sometimes, and you are the only person here with me. I'm fighting for my life and taking multiple medications. Most of these medications have numerous adverse side effects.

Do not make or give me any food, gift, etc. that has a strong odor.

Don't give up on me.

Don't ever tell me that I am helpless; encourage me instead.

Don't make me feel guilty because you are taking care of me. I already feel like I'm imposing on you. Do it from your heart.

What Friends and Family Members Can Know and Do

Come and visit, but don't expect to be entertained.

Cheer me up.

Think of fun activities that do not require too much energy. Engaging in group conversation is exhausting.

Send cards with your heartfelt expressions of support and hope.

Send gifts of books.

Send crystals that symbolize light.

Go to high tea with me.

Wear pink to show your support.

Shave your head for support.

Give a gift of the Fruit of the Month Club. My friend Scott from Seattle signed me up, and I received my first box of delicious peaches just two days after my first chemo treatment. I remember how juicy and perfect they were.

Offer to help with organizational and administrative tasks, especially anything that involves dealing with the insurance company.

Take me shopping for girly stuff. You can never get too much pampering, no matter how you feel. Do send small gifts of tea, fruit, books, audio CDs, and movies. Comedies are great.

When I have the energy, spend time with me, playing board games or cards.

Pray for me often.

Invite me to your home and include me as though I will always be around.

Follow up with me. Don't expect me to call you. Just make it a point to check on me; my memory and energy levels are being severely taxed by my treatment.

Send me a card or note, an inspirational book, or music.

Use this as an opportunity for your own growth as well.

Do something fun for or with me after the completion of each chemo session.

Don't assume this is the end for me. Make sure you include me in as many of your social activities as possible; I may not be able to make them all, but I appreciate that you are thinking of me.

Don't ever say you are sorry that I have cancer. That makes me feel sad and makes me wonder if I am supposed to feel sorry for myself. Instead, just ask if there is anything you can do to help me. Offer to bring food, take me out to a movie, or drive me somewhere. These are some of the things that I appreciate most.

Don't send flowers. People who are going through chemo can be easily nauseated by strong scents and odors.

Don't wear perfume, lotion, or anything with a scent.

Don't expect me to have long phone conversations. It takes a lot more energy than you might think.

Ask me if you would like to touch my bald head.

Keep me away from crowded places.

Don't tell me to be strong. I'm doing the best I can.

I know that I look bad; I don't need to be reminded.

Don't feel pity for me, because I can see it in your eyes.

Appreciate me for the accomplishments I've made so far. Don't criticize me for being weak.

Don't label me.

Most of the time, I enjoy your touch; I won't break if you touch me.

I can't make you feel better about me or yourself when you are sad; it's difficult enough for me to keep my own spirits high.

What the Medical Community Can Know and Do

Refer to me by my name and look at me when you talk to me.

Encourage me to get a second opinion.

Properly introduce yourself and help me to feel comfortable with your competence.

Give me hope. Don't discuss me as though I am some lab animal.

Spend time talking with me and explaining the various (and many) procedures that I will be going through and how they may affect me physically and emotionally.

Encourage me to ask questions.

Be gentle with me if you are poking me with a needle; my body has been through so much already.

Smile.

Listen to me.

Allow me to have an opinion.

Have someone from your office follow up with me at home to make sure the procedure went well.

Write down instructions for me. I may forget some of the details.

Have a sense of humor.

Pay attention when you are dealing with my body. Be completely present.

Give me all of my options and the side effects. Offer solutions and allow me to participate in decisions about my treatment.

Take your time when you deliver not so good news, and be prepared to respond to my emotions.

Think *How would I want my daughter or wife to be treated if they were going through this?*

Don't write me off.

Treat me like a person—not a subject, a number, or a statistical example.

Quoting depressing facts to me isn't helpful. I'm intelligent and can read the statistics myself; they are all readily available.

Don't make me wait for hours to meet with you; I'm already fearful and often simply don't feel like being anywhere, much less in a waiting room.

I'm already feeling depressed; be gentle when you break the bad news to me.

What Employers and Coworkers Can Know and Do

Be my advocate.

Provide me with assurance that my job is not in danger.

Offer to help me deal with the insurance company; they are very often bureaucratic and have no empathy. It is very stressful trying to manage all the paperwork required by the insurance companies. They will treat me better if you are supporting me and acting on my behalf.

Have someone from HR follow up with me periodically to make sure the insurance companies are treating me well.

Help me go through this period by modifying my work responsibilities.

Give me flexibility and permission to work from home on an as-needed basis.

Treat me with respect and dignity.

Help me understand various FMLA options. (FMLA was a great option for me.)

Treat me like I'm part of your team.

Reassure me that my illness is not in any way going to work against me.

Be fair.

Don't discriminate against me because I am ill. I am not slow; I am just weak. It takes a lot of energy to be here.

Don't give me responsibilities that are physically challenging. The chemo is already making me weak.

Don't test me or put me on performance evaluation because I have not been able to perform as my usual self. These are very difficult times and I'm doing the best I can. The medications have many side effects.

I'm proud of the fight that I'm going through, but I don't want to be a mascot, especially when I haven't completely healed physically and emotionally yet. Treat me with the same respect and dignity as you treat others.

Noise, light, scent, and crowds are difficult for me physically and sometimes emotionally. Offer to help relocate my office if needed.

Don't judge me.

When I feel comfortable to share my experience or feelings, I will; please don't put me in the position of feeling obligated to explain my situation.

Multitasking is difficult for me while going through chemo; please be patient and understanding if I seem distracted or not completely on top of things.

Don't be afraid.

Feel free to stop by and chat with me about my experience. Some of my most pleasant work experiences involved managers stopping by periodically to check on me and assure me of how much respect they had for me for showing up to work considering all my challenges.

Don't be afraid to ask how things are going; I'll gladly share what I feel I can at that time.

About the Author

Erin grew up in Tehran, Iran. At seventeen, she came to the United States, where she learned to speak English and studied systems engineering. She went onto graduate school for a Master of Arts in Computer Applications, and she is currently working as an information technology program manager for a successful energy management company.

Erin is a ten-year survivor of breast cancer and a believer in celebrating life, being positive, using humor to deal with stress, and giving hope to others. She has been participating in the Susan G. Komen Race for the Cure since long before her own diagnosis. She has raised thousands of dollars for the Susan G. Komen Foundation and consistently earned a spot on the Pink Honor Roll, which recognizes the top fundraisers in South Florida. Erin served as an honorary chair of Komen in 2008, and received the Pink Warrior Award in recognition of her community service.

Acknowledgments

Dad, all my life, your love has meant the world to me. You have always made me feel so special. Thank you, Mom, for giving me the gifts of courage, strength, and tenacity. You left us too soon to see me get well. You are my hero.

Alex, thank you for looking after everyone and thanks for sending me the box from Harrods. The goodies are all gone, but I still have the box. Farzaneh, you are my angel. You pulled my spirit out of the swamp when I was at my lowest. Jay, thanks for being such a great friend and brother to me all these years. DJ, you are very special and kind, and can make me laugh when I am down.

Thank you, Jim, for being there and keeping me company and being my primary support during the worst time of my life. Your positivity and encouragement meant the world to me. We will always be bonded together.

Thank you, Ladan Mirhashemi, for your personal assistance and social media expertise during the last part of this project. It made a difference.

My dear aunt Ame Joon, it was because of you that I got involved with the Komen Foundation more than twenty years ago. Every race I did for the Komen was in your memory.

Dee, thank you for embracing me with your artistic spirit. Thank you, Dan, for lifting me when I was at my lowest. You reminded me how it is all about energy. Thank you, Nancy, for being always a great friend—you've always been there for me. I appreciate having you accompany me when I got the worst news at Mayo. Thank you, Scott, for signing me up for the Fruit of the Month Club during chemo and coming to see me during my illness. You are as close as it gets to a soul mate. Thank you, Tim and Donna, for your support all these years. Thank you, Denise, for bringing light into my life by painting with me, encouraging me, and showing me what I can do. Thank you, Ellen, for being such a great confidant and mommy to Jelly Bean, and helping me balance life and work. Thank you, Sheila, for bringing sunshine into my life and helping me get well. Thank you, Vicky and Susan, for the food and groceries when I needed them the most. Thank you, Suzanne, for always being there for us with your cheerful smile and positive attitude.

Thank you, Donna, Glenn, Erika, and Frank, for giving me the most needed motivation, and for helping review and proofread my book.

Thank you, John and Cecilia, for helping me become healthy in mind, body, and soul, all these years and for all the years to come.

Thank you, Patti, for waking me up and showing me the way.

Thanks, Michele Donahue, for reading the first draft and providing such great feedback.

Thank you, Doug Murray, for meeting me and Jelly Bean for our photo shoot during such early morning hours on your weekend. You are so nice.

Thank you, Mayo Clinic, for giving me the best possible care. You are a sanctuary for so many people in the world. Thanks to Dr. Jacobson and his OR nurse, Diane. Thanks to Dr. Knoegen, Dr. Grant, and Dr. Raymond. Special thanks to my favorite oncologist, Dr. Long, for all of your care the last ten years. You left this world too soon. I will miss you every time I visit the Mayo Clinic.

Thank you, Dr. Gazze, for being there for me and giving me the best care and advice possible.

Thank you to my cancer support team for being great sisters to me. Thank you, Komen Foundation, for elevating me and for helping me to maintain a positive outlook and understand that there were countless possibilities in my future.

Thank you, Patricia Sands, for giving me such great advice, for sharing your experience with me, and for introducing me to Carrie and David.

Thank you, Carrie Spencer, for your patience and artistic input in designing my book cover.

Thank you, David Bernardi, for your editorial guidance and vision. I am still in awe that we did it.

Thanks to my employer and all my colleagues and managers who have supported me.

And of course, without my faithful dog Jelly Bean, I wouldn't have been as happy as I was while going through such darkness.

Thank you, God, for bringing me to this point in life. I'm writing this book with the utmost intention, to help shine light for souls lost in darkness.

If you would like to share your own story of survival, or if you wish to learn more about the Susan G. Komen Race for the Cure, please visit http://ihavesurvived.com.

You may also write to me at

Erin Arbabha
PO Box #2293
Stuart, FL 34995

Tribute to Susan G. Komen Race for the Cure

Komen is vision, courage, support, responsibility, hope, promise, cure, love, togetherness, celebration, research, community, and education. Nancy Goodman Brinker's sister, Susan G. Komen, died from breast cancer in 1980. Nancy founded the Susan G. Komen Race for the Cure fundraising organization to raise money for breast cancer research. Komen Race for the Cure is the world's largest and most successful fundraising event for breast cancer.

I was first introduced to the Komen Race for the Cure in Des Moines, Iowa, in 1992 when I participated to honor the memory of my aunt who had recently died from breast cancer at the young age of forty-two. I recall the day, so many people of all ages wearing pink and celebrating. I took up running just to be able to participate in the Race for the Cure. I woke up early, excited about participating.

Every year thereafter, my friends and I look forward to this event. We make a date to participate in the race and then sometimes go for brunch. We laugh, cry, celebrate survivors, and honor those who are no longer with us. It is always an emotional day, but uplifting at the same time, as we acknowledge that we haven't given up and that we are all helping to do something about it.

After my breast cancer, I started participating in the race as a survivor, enjoying the experience and the rites of camaraderie among the other survivors. I remember my first year as a survivor, how emotional I was, but seeing all the people who had survived twenty or more years after their original diagnoses gave me hope.

When I began to feel better, I wanted to give something back, so I began fundraising every year. During my first year of fundraising, my goal was to raise $200; I created a website at work, and within a week, I had already exceeded my goal, so I increased it to $500. It was so easy to raise money. All I had to do was ask, and many generous people would contribute. Sometimes, it was only a few dollars; in other cases, people donated thousands. But it all added up very quickly, and all of it was going toward the cause.

After that first time, I was no longer shy about asking for money. Each year, I found that I was able to raise more and more for the cause. I started asking friends, neighbors, former employers, and even Facebook friends. I have been in the top fifty fundraisers consistently in South Florida for the last few years. I was asked to be an honorary chair of Komen for my company in 2008 and was awarded the Pink Warrior Award in 2011. This award is given to those who have performed outstanding community service, including fundraising.

There is no greater joy than service and being able to give something back. It has been my pleasure and honor to participate, in my own small way, to help Komen reach its goals and work toward fulfilling its vision; I will continue to do so.

Please visit http://www.komen.org to learn more about the Komen Foundation and consider joining us in our race for the cure.

26733173R00130

Made in the USA
Middletown, DE
05 December 2015